Ambushed
BY GRACE

Ambushed
BY GRACE

HELP & HOPE ON THE
CAREGIVING JOURNEY

SHELLY BEACH

DISCOVERY HOUSE
PUBLISHERS®

Feeding the Soul with the Word of God

Discovery House Publishers is affiliated with RBC Ministries,
Grand Rapids, Michigan.

Discovery House books are distributed to the trade exclusively by
Barbour Publishing, Inc., Uhrichsville, Ohio.

Requests for permission to quote from this book should be directed to:
Permissions Department, Discovery House Publishers, P.O. Box 3566,
Grand Rapids, MI 49501.

Scripture quotations are from the *Holy Bible, New International Version®.
NIV®.* Copyright © 1973, 1978, 1984 by International Bible Society.
Used by permission of Zondervan. All rights reserved.

Interior design by Sherri L. Hoffman

Library of Congress Cataloging-in-Publication Data

Beach, Shelly.
    Ambushed by grace : help, hope, and heart transformation on
the caregiving journey by / Shelly Beach.
        p. cm.
    ISBN 978-1-57293-242-5
    1. Caregivers—Religious life.   2. Caring—Religious aspects—
Christianity.   3. Grace (Theology)   I. Title.
        BV4910.9.B425 2007
        248.8'8—dc22   2008038626

Printed in the United States of America

09 10 11 12 13 / DP / 10 9 8 7 6 5 4 3

To my parents,

Paul and Phyllis Burke,
whose faithfulness in loving their Lord,
each other,
and family and friends
has been my example, encouragement, and illustration of
Jesus' love.

And to my parents-in-law,

Norman and Marian Beach,
whose heritage of godly service and love of family
have shaped generations for eternity.

Contents

Acknowledgments

My deep and heartfelt thanks to the many people who helped encourage me along the journey to the completion of this book:

To the wonderful family at Discovery House Publishers, and especially my editor extraordinaire, Annette Gysen, and publisher Carol Holquist, who have helped make writing this book a joy from start to finish.

To my dear Guilders, whose encouragement is threaded through each page: Ann Byle, Angela Blycker, Tracy Groot, Sharon Carrns, Alison Hodgson, Cynthia Beach, Julie Johnson, and Lorilee Craker.

My unending thanks for the ministry of Blythefield Hills Baptist Church for the instruction, counsel, and teaching they pour into my life that makes my writing possible.

To my husband Dan and children Jessica and Nate, always supportive cheerleaders and who have lived caregiving from the inside out.

And to my dear father, Paul Burke, who faithfully modeled caregiving until my mother's final breath.

But he said to me,
"My grace is sufficient for you, for my power is made perfect in weakness."
Therefore I will boast all the more gladly about my weaknesses,
so that Christ's power may rest on me.
That is why, for Christ's sake,
I delight in weaknesses,
in insults,
in hardships,
in persecutions,
in difficulties.
For when I am weak, then I am strong.

2 CORINTHIANS 12:9–10

Chapter One

Dipping Your Hand in the Mason Jar

EXPECTATIONS AND REALITIES OF
THE CAREGIVING JOURNEY

"You don't know my mother. She's like nobody you've ever met. I can tell you one thing for certain: when she's old and senile, there's no way on earth I'll ever take care of her. She's impossible. My sisters and I have already decided she's going into a nursing home because none of us can put up with her. We think Dad might have arranged his heart attack because it was an easier way out.

"We've all got families and jobs. I've got diabetes to contend with, and I've got to keep my own health in mind, right? And I can hardly imagine what would happen to my marriage if we moved her in. Bill and I don't even have a guest room. Right now we barely have time to get our kids to youth group and practices, and Bill's job keeps him traveling all the time, so he'd be no help at all. I could never put up with the demands Mom places on everybody and remain sane. There's no way on earth I could ever take care of her. I don't have it in me, and I get sick just thinking about it.

"I don't know how you do it, I really don't. Your life has revolved around taking care of your father-in-law for years. You even quit your full-time job. Is that what I'm supposed to do? Put my life on hold, sacrifice everything, let my mother take over my life?

"Is that what 'good' daughters do? Just lay it all down and pretend to be spiritual about it?"

Stacy

*I*n her book *Traveling Mercies*, Anne Lamott said, "I do not at all understand the mystery of grace—only that it meets us where we are but does not leave us where it found us."

When I began caregiving six years ago, I did not expect to embark upon a journey of grace. I expected to learn of service and sacrifice, to explore new facets of patience and tolerance, love and forgiveness, but I did not expect to be changed at the core of my being. I did not know then what I know now—that caregiving, by the power of God's grace, can be a work of redemption powerful enough to reverberate into the hearts of those around us.

I did not expect caregiving to strip me down and reveal my motives, my passions, my agendas, and my priorities. I did not expect it to pin me to the mat in a spiritual wrestling match, sweaty and writhing, until I saw for the first time what it meant to live like Jesus—to selflessly, passionately pour life into life without regard for self.

Caregiving is a gift that comes wrapped with the price tag still dangling, a tag that reads *Inestimable Cost, Eternal Value*. To make caregiving simply a task is a distortion of its purpose; rather, it is a divine appointment, a redemptive encounter, and an act of worship. God presents this gift to us, as He does all His gifts, as an opportunity to conform us to the image of His Son, to draw us more tightly to His heart as we learn to depend on Him. It's as if His desire is to bind us to himself in a spiritual three-legged race until our pace matches His own, and the means He uses to entwine our body to His is the care of our loved one. It wasn't until I learned to relinquish my stride to His, to abandon control of my direction, and to match the rhythm of my pace to His that I discovered He was carrying me like a child standing upon her father's shoes, clinging to his legs as she stared into his face, waiting for the next step.

You may be well down the path in your caregiving journey, or perhaps you don't know where to place your feet for the first steps.

Let me assure you, wherever you are in your journey, you aren't alone. God has called you, and He will carry you as you learn to relinquish your stride to His, despite your fears or misgivings. No one loves your dear one more than God himself. You're in partnership with the God of the universe to cherish and minister to one of His unique image bearers, whether he or she is a glowing saint, a salty sinner, or somewhere in between.

God will meet you where you are, and He will faithfully bear you up for every step. You are encompassed on every side by His presence. Your hope is eternal, rooted in the character of God himself.

Be prepared to be ambushed by grace on the journey ahead. God intends to use caregiving to change the very heart of you. He desires to transform you by the mystery of grace into the image of His beloved Son as you learn how to minister to your loved one's needs, ease that needy one's pain, pour balm on family wounds, and work at the challenge of healthy boundaries. It will be a difficult journey, to be sure. But God will meet you where you are, and He will faithfully bear you up for every step. You are encompassed on every side by His presence. Your hope is eternal, rooted in the character of God himself.

When I wrote the words of this manuscript months ago, I didn't know I'd be making the last edits for publication of them as I sat beside my mother's still and silent body during her final hours on earth. I didn't know God would graciously choose to end her suffering from Alzheimer's disease with a sudden fall and brain injury, allowing her to sleep her way to glory surrounded by the loving ministrations of her family. I didn't realize my own words would point me to the truth of God's Word during the moments when I needed it most.

But God had it planned from the beginning—His plan for my mother's final breath and His plan to comfort my heart with the reality of His presence as her pulse stilled beneath my fingers.

"For I know the plans I have for you,"
declares the Lord,
"plans to prosper you and not to harm you,
plans to give you hope and a future.
Then you will call upon me
and come and pray to me,
and I will listen to you.

You will seek me and find me when you seek me with all your heart."

JEREMIAH 29:11–13

The mystery of caregiving is the mystery of grace—the grace that God will not leave us where He finds us, and that when the journey is over, if grace has done its transforming work, we will find ourselves lost in the reality of His love for us more and more along the way.

This is a book that offers practical advice, Web sites, phone numbers, and wisdom from experts in the fields of geriatrics and family counseling. But first and foremost, it is a book intended to draw you into the Word and to sensitize you to the work of the Spirit of God in your life.

Dipping Your Hand in the Mason Jar: Startling Realities of Caregiving

When I was thirteen, my ninety-year-old grandmother moved into our home. Grandma Burke was from the Old Country and left her family to move to "Visconsin" from Sweden at the age of fifteen. At the ripe age of ninety, she became my roommate. Grandma did not share my affinity for the Beatles or bell-bottoms, and I did not share her affinity for warm prune juice or smacking her gums when she removed her teeth. My life was marked by the mortal fear that she would hightail it off to glory some night, and I would open my eyes in the morning and find myself staring at a corpse.

One morning in the pre-dawn darkness, I lay in my bed with my eyes squeezed shut against the taunting specter of death in the twin bed across the room just inches from my own. As I steeled myself for a much-needed foray to the bathroom, I made the decision to avert my eyes from Grandma's potentially lifeless form until I could flee to the bathroom and sneak quietly back. In the darkness, I reached for my glasses at their familiar spot on the bedside stand, but to my surprise, I found my hand unexpectedly plunging into a mason jar of

Roadside Rest

SCRIPTURE FOR MEDITATION

I pray that out of his glorious riches he may strengthen you with power through his Spirit in your inner being (Ephesians 3:16).

icy water. As I panicked, my fingers clamped down, and I quite unexpectedly latched on to Grandma's teeth and pulled them, dripping, from the mouth of the jar.

Something inside me must have snapped as I hurled Grandma's dentures across the room with the force of an Olympic shot-putter. My screams would have killed a less sturdy ninety-year-old, but Grandma Burke was a Swede who had raised ten children during the Depression on salt pork and lutefisk. She lived another year before quietly succumbing to pneumonia, but it was shortly after the Morning of the Flinging Teeth that her health went into a decline, and my parents moved her to a nursing home.

Many of us come to caregiving in a similar fashion, with our eyes clenched shut against the specter of death that hovers just beyond our vision as we grope in the darkness for something, anything, that will help us find our way on our journey. Then comes the moment when our hand plunges into the mason jar, and we realize we've grasped something we hadn't quite expected, something we may have never before had to face at close range. In that moment we may ask ourselves, *What have I gotten into? What am I doing here, anyway?* In the early days of my caregiving journey, I wasn't really sure.

The Teeth in My Hand:
My Caregiving Journey

Dan and I were both raised in households where grandparents were part of the family structure. Dan's grandmother had suffered from a form of dementia, most likely Alzheimer's, and amicable neighbors had graciously collected her and brought her home when she occasionally wandered away. Caring for aging grandparents was part of the family culture Dan and I shared, like tithing and not swearing and not going to movies—or at least not telling your parents you did. So we always believed it would be our responsibility to care for our parents someday, possibly in our home. But we had never expected those responsibilities to begin when our kids were still young enough to enjoy eating Play-Doh—just four and six.

Roadside Realities

In 1990, the ratio of caregivers to elderly persons needing care was one to eleven; by 2050, that ratio will be reduced to one to four.

The National Caregivers' Association, "Family Caregiving Statistics," 2000.

Norman came to live with us for the first time in 1983 because of severe malnutrition due to food allergies. His condition was so dire that he had lost his ability to recognize us or to speak. He lived with us for four months while we sought medical treatment and nourished him back to health. Six years after his first recovery he returned, with only 117 pounds clinging to his six-foot-two-inch frame. Doctors feared pancreatic cancer, but once again malnutrition was the cause. This time he lived with us for six months while he regained physical and mental strength and we found an allergist whose treatment allowed him to eat normally for the remainder of his life.

Then in 2000, when Norman's friends called again and told us of his depression and anxiety, we knew that short-term interventions were no longer an option. Our only recourse was to have him move in with us or his daughter Sue. Since he had already lived with us twice and elder care was excellent in Iowa, where Dan and I were living at the time, the choice seemed obvious to everyone in the family. So I squeezed my eyes shut and plunged my hand into the mason jar.

Norman would live with us for four-and-a-half years. During that time, he suffered from a number of physical and mental illnesses, including obsessive-compulsive disorder, depression, and Parkinson's disease. He went through periods of care in hospitals and rehab centers, always returning to our home when he was well enough. During those same years, my mother, who lived with my father back in Michigan, slipped into the abyss of Alzheimer's, and my dad began to manifest strange cardiac and neurological symptoms. My life became a surreal choreography of medical emergency flights, doctors' appointments, hospitalizations, and rehabilitations with Norman, interspersed with my own ER visits and hospital stays from a quirky brain lesion that had nearly taken my life in 1999 and left me one fry short of a Happy Meal with my own physical health. For years it seemed I was either racing to someone's side for

> ### *Roadside Assistance*
>
> When you don't know where to begin in your search for elder-care resources, your local Area Agency on Aging is a great starting point. Look in the blue pages of the phonebook under "Guide to Human Services," or check out the Web at www.n4a.org.

an emergency room crisis or heading off for my own. By the time Dad Beach had lived with us a few years, most of the doctors I met thought I was a doctor myself. I knew I was certainly willing to sign up for a medical convention somewhere in the Caribbean.

The Dilemma of Drippy Dentures:
The Conflict of Expectations and Realities

Then in 2004, God suddenly flung open doors that allowed us to move back to Michigan to be near my parents, and I raced through them with all the speed my weary, worn-out body could muster. For a month or two I allowed my spirit to exhale. I found my dream job at a Christian university, but it didn't take long for reality to slap me in the rear, like a screen door with a broken spring. Finding new doctors for Norman had made me best friends with my Excedrin bottle, and even though Dan was helping more with his father's appointments, it seemed like all the doctors we had found had conspired to work out of offices on the opposite side of the city. My parents lived almost an hour from our new home, and I could explode a blood pressure cuff just talking about their medical needs. Every day I drove to work I could think of five reasons to be at home caring for Norman and ten more to be in Muskegon caring for Mom and Dad. The home health care we had worked so hard to arrange in Iowa had evaporated in Michigan, and Norman was alone at home for hours at a time. Had we sacrificed Dan's father's care for my mom's and dad's? It seemed that no matter where I was or what I was doing, I felt guilty. My migraines were becoming more frequent and more intense, and I had put my neurologist on speed-dial. There were days I looked at the drippy mess of my life and wanted to fling the problems and frustrations across the room like Grandma's teeth, crawl back into my bed, and pull up the covers.

Then one afternoon the picture changed. Norman took a fall while Dan was helping him in the bathroom. Before a week had passed, he took another tumble, this time while we were at work. That was the day we knew the inevitable had arrived—we couldn't keep Norman safe in our home any longer. The Parkinson's had progressed too far. We knew that this time when Dad Beach left our home, he wouldn't return. He knew it, too. And he knew that we had done all we could for as long as we could to keep him in our home.

We grieved a loss the day we moved Norman into the Michigan Home for Veterans, less than ten miles from our house, where he lived for eleven months before Jesus called him home to really rest. But we already knew that caring for loved ones doesn't mean they must live in your home. Often their best care is provided in their own home, in a nursing home, in assisted living, or in another scenario. Even though it wasn't easy, moving Norman into the Veteran's Home forced us to transition and re-evaluate once again. The day after Norman moved, Dan and I prepared his room for my parents. Soon after that, I quit my job at the university and began freelancing so I could have more flexibility to help share my parents' care with my brother, Paul, and his wife, Sheryl. Right now in the morning hours, my folks are stirring in the room next to me, and that means that for today, at least, I'm blessed to care for them in my home.

The Stacy in All of Us:
The Trap of Expectations

At the beginning of this chapter, we heard Stacy's voice, which, to one degree or another, echoes the fears we all share— voices that tell us to fight for our rights, to exert our power, to push our way to the front of the crowd. Voices of culture that tell us it's our responsibility to look out for ourselves, to protect our interests, to make life as prosperous and pleasurable as we can. After all, we have spouses and children to consider, health insurance and retirement plans to protect. And the financial realities of caregiving alone are stark. Eventually, 12 percent of the one-third to one-half of caregivers who are employed outside the home quit their jobs to provide care full-time.[1] And the vast majority of these caregivers are women. I'm one of them.

Josh Montez, in the August 22, 2006, issue of *Family News in Focus* reports on one of the voices calling out to Stacy from popular culture. The BBC host of "Women's Hour," Jenni Murray, is a media figure who has spent her life seeking liberation and independence. Recently she announced that her aging mother has late-stage Parkinson's disease. Murray shared her concern for becoming "trapped" in caring for her dependent parents in an article that states that she "does not want to look after her sick and aging mother and plans to end her own life when she becomes a burden." Murray aired her views on a BBC television program called "Don't Get Me Started" that highlighted the growing philosophy of the obligation to die, an opinion held by leading thinkers in bioethics who argue that elderly and ill patients have the obligation to relieve pressure on their families and the health care system.[2]

> ## *Roadside Realities*
>
> According to the National Alliance for Caregiving, 73 percent of sandwich-generation caregivers are women who will spend 18 years caring for an elderly parent and will often leave the workforce with reduced 401(k) and pension plans.

---

1. *Family Caregiver Alliance Fact Sheet*: Work and Eldercare, 2006.
2. Hilary White, *BBC Feminist's Sordid Suicide Pact Made Public*. LifeSite. http://www.lifesitenews.com/ldn/2006/aug/06081503.html).

Standing in stark contrast to Jenni Murray is Robertson McQuilken, former president of Columbia Bible College. When Robertson's wife, Muriel, was diagnosed with Alzheimer's, he chose an early retirement so he could minister at her side until her death. "Love takes the sting out of duty," Robertson states in his book *A Promise Kept* (Tyndale, 1998). "Here's my lover. What can I do to make her life easier?"

The Gift of the Mason Jar: The Awakening

When Norman first came to stay with us, I was startled to discover I was once again a child huddled beneath the covers with her eyes squeezed shut against the unknown, against disease and the descent toward death that lay in the room across the hall. I knew that in a practical yet almost symbolic way, Norman and I had been wed. I was the woman who ministered to his daily needs. I was the woman who would accompany him to his death, and I was afraid—of what I would lose, of what I would discover about myself, of what I would be asked to lay down as we walked that path together. Waking up that first morning with Norman on the other side of our bedroom door, my spirit was plunged into the narrow neck of a mason jar, and I felt the unexpected bite of the cold water against my will. God was about to begin a new thing in Norman and in our family. I was about to begin a journey that would teach me truth—about myself and about God's sufficiency—at a deep level.

Power in an Open Hand: The Inestimable Gifts

Caregiving is difficult—for us, for our families, for our loved ones. It is messy work. We must expect tension and turmoil, but in that tension and turmoil, we can expect redemption, reconciliation, and affirmation. Caregiving is not a means to a promised end, but because the process reflects the character of Christ himself, we can be assured it will transform us. And if we approach caregiving as a journey into our own souls, asking God to reveal himself to us, we will be rewarded by an avalanche of grace. Philippians 4:19 promises us that "My God will meet all your needs according to his glorious riches in Christ Jesus."

Caregiving teaches us to see what is precious and valuable in life. It teaches us what it means to live out commitment and honor. It gives us the opportunity to love someone better who we may have struggled to love in the past. It gives us the opportunity to demonstrate that God is sufficient and that He is a God who redeems.

Caregiving is the hardest work we will ever do because it demands that we love as Christ loved, sacrificing our time, our jobs, our commitments, our friendships, and our health, while standing against the tide of culture. We will be asked to lay down expectations of fairness and to expect stress in our family relationships. We will be asked to crawl onto the altar, knowing God's desire is to hone us and mold us into the character of His Son. We must be willing to search our hearts and focus the light of the Word upon our self-talk, our motives, and our actions. Caregiving is a journey into the character of Christ.

The Call of the Mason Jar: The Call to the Journey

The quality of our caregiving is not measured by geography—whether it is given in our home, from a distance, or in a nursing home. It is measured by how we reflect the character of Christ. Caregiving will not look the same for every person or every family. It has as many shapes and forms as there are needs. True strength in caregiving lies in the paradox that our weaknesses are made strong through the sufficiency of God.

The call to caregiving is the call to dip your hand in the mason jar—to abandon yourself to spiritual awakening through the power of redeeming grace. It is a call to suffer, to sacrifice, and to serve. It is a call to abandonment and tears, to hardships and difficulties.

It is a glorious call to be conformed to the image of Christ and to join the God of the universe in ministering grace and mercy to one of His image bearers. It is a call to become a splash of magnificent magenta or burst of brilliant orange on God's eternal canvas.

And what could possibly be more exciting than that?

Prayer

Most loving Father, in this moment birth in me the desire to be changed in the deep places of my heart that are so difficult for me to see. May your Holy Spirit move in me, stirring me, convicting me of sin, showing me my vanities, ambitions, fears, pride. Lord, may I be willing to lay down my expectations of fairness and my need to have others come through for me. May I be committed to being conformed to the image of your Son and be willing, like Him, to suffer, to sacrifice, and to serve.

May I desire brokenness and emptiness in order to know you more and to know what it means to be fulfilled in you. Heal the broken places in me, and change my heart. Renew a right spirit within me. Give me the vision of myself that you have for me. Thank you for your relentless passion for me and the ways that, even now, your Holy Spirit is moving within my life to change me.

Father, make me a minister of your grace and mercy to others. Let me rest in your overwhelming love poured out for me and your provision for each moment of my life.

Thank you for the blessings you lavish over my life and my loved one's life. In the precious name of Jesus, amen.

Meditation and Personal Application Questions

1. Can you relate to Stacy's feelings? In what ways?
2. How do you apply 2 Corinthians 12:9–10 to Stacy's circumstances? How would you apply this passage to your caregiving circumstances?

3. Read Philippians 2:5–8. This passage tells us that our attitude should be the same as Jesus Christ's, who took on the form of a servant. How does this Scripture align with Robertson McQuilken's approach to caring for his wife?

4. How do we as caregivers balance servanthood in our caregiving with the practical realities of life? In the book *Boundaries*, Dr. Henry Cloud and Dr. John Townsend present a number of principles, among them:

   - God desires compassion and not sacrifice. Don't take on too many responsibilities.
   - It's okay to say no to people. Being Christlike does not mean we must always comply with someone's wishes.
   - It's healthy to establish boundaries around our God-given desires and to nourish the dreams and aspirations the Spirit has implanted within us.

5. In what ways do you feel God may desire to redeem you and change you through caregiving? What do you think may be required of you in order for this change to take place?

Scripture for Further Meditation

Brokenness: Psalm 51:1, 6
Commitment: Psalm 37:3–7; Matthew 10:38–39
Compassion: Psalm 86:15

Should Your Parents Move In with You?

Consult appendix 2 for this helpful resource to help you assess your individual family circumstances.

"The most important one," [of all the commandments]
answered Jesus, "is this:
'Hear, O Israel, the Lord our God, the Lord is one.
Love the Lord your God with all your heart
and with all your soul
and with all your mind
and with all your strength.'
The second is this: 'Love your neighbor as yourself.'
There is no commandment greater than these."

MARK 12:29–31

Chapter Two

Why *Kum-Bah-Yah* Is Not Enough

IMPERATIVES OF THE DOUBLE-LOVE COMMAND

"Things got complicated when my parents' health began to deteriorate," Mona shares. "My father had Parkinson's and my mother had a broken hip that required her to use a walker. I was driving hundreds of miles every week to care for them, to cook and grocery shop, and because of my health, I was usually on crutches myself.

"For a short time my parents tried living in a retirement community, but then Dad's needs grew to more than Mom could deal with. All the staff counseled us against moving my parents in to live with us. They said it was crazy with my health problems. But there was nothing I wanted more than to bring them home to care for them. If things got difficult, they'd be in my home, and I wouldn't be driving all the time."

Louie, Mona's husband, is quick to respond. "People have to realize that walking out these decisions isn't romantic. It's always messy. But you make decisions and press forward. Mona wanted to honor her parents this way because of their life of honor. Honor doesn't always look the same for everyone, but our choice is one way I honored my wife."

As months slipped into years and Mona's parents' needs progressed, people often asked how long she would continue in-home care. Her answer was always the same.

"Until I've given more than I've received."

Louie and Mona

Several years into our marriage, Dan arrived home one afternoon wearing a look that told me he was about to impart some item of new and wonderful information. I'd learned, after a few Christmases of bleakly wrapped Micro-Go-Rounds and Chia Pets, that my husband sometimes defined "new and wonderful" differently from how I did. In that era of life when newly invented Velcro fasteners on children's tennis shoes rocked my world, I was willing to set my expectations pretty low. But then low expectations had become a subliminal pattern of life for me in many areas, including my spiritual life. I just hadn't had the courage to admit it at the time.

Dan's childish grin told me he expected me to share in his excitement.

"Just a few miles from our house, down a gravel back road, there's—can you believe this—an *actual* artesian well."

An *actual* artesian well.

I had been secretly hoping to hear the word *mega-mall*, but I tried to muster up a bit of excitement for the well thing. After all, city water meant monthly bills, and well water would probably be free. My mind searched for economic advantages... something. And, after all, Dan promised it was an *actual* artesian well, whatever that meant.

I tried to envision what an actual artesian well would look like. The word *artesian* sounded, well, so artsy. My mind stirred up visions of a Victorian garden at the end of a winding forest path. Flowers and trees were laid out artfully around a graceful minigeyser that shot a rainbow mist into the air that cascaded back to earth into a rippling pool. People gathered around the perimeter and dipped earthen vases and brass urns into the sweet, refreshing water, and women drifted about the scene gowned in flowing dresses and greeting one another with English accents.

That's what an artesian well *sounded* like it should look like, to my way of thinking. But if my vision was accurate, I wouldn't fit into the picture. A person would practically need an English pedigree to show up. But reality set in, and without a flowing dress or the trace of an English accent, on the following Saturday morning, I stashed our two children with my parents, and Dan and I set out to find the well. And since we were low on vases and urns, we tossed three plastic gallon jugs in the back seat of our yellow Gremlin.

It didn't take long for us to discover the well, just a few feet off a dirt road and beyond a shallow ditch not far from Michigan Highway 24. My idyllic Victorian garden vaporized as I surveyed a patch of underbrush near a scabbed oak that listed to the southwest. It took me a few *actual* minutes to recognize that what I was actually looking at was an *actual* well: a nondescript three-inch galvanized pipe protruding horizontally from a mound in the earth with a steady stream of water pulsating quietly to the dirt beneath.

No geysers. No gardens.

Just a plain old pipe stuck in the ground. Just dirt and mud and a nondescript stream of water that looked like the flow from our garden hose. I don't know if Dan sensed my inner sigh.

But despite my disappointment, we bent down and filled our dented plastic jugs. And there beneath the scabbed oak, with our sneakers planted in the sodden soil, we took our first sip and stood, stunned.

What bubbled up from the depths was better than anything we had ever tasted. It not only slaked our thirst but was so delicious that after that day we refused to drink our city water again. And best of all, it was free.

The water from our well was so good, in fact, that we couldn't keep it to ourselves. Like Dan's friend at school who had told him about the well, we told others, and they came, too.

> ## *Roadside Rest*
>
> ### SCRIPTURE FOR MEDITATION
>
> Jesus answered, "Everyone who drinks this water will be thirsty again, but whoever drinks the water I give him will never thirst. Indeed, the water I give him will become in him a spring of water welling up to eternal life" (John 4:13).

Week after week. Month after month. Year after year.

Because, after all, we had found an artesian well. An *actual* artesian well.

It was our well. Despite its moat of mud and barricade of brambles, it had become ours at the first sip.

My Life as a *Kum-Bah-Yah* Christian: When We're Disappointed

Without quite knowing it, in the artesian well years of my life, when my children were small, I became content with smallness in other areas of my life. I learned to set my expectations low and to avert my gaze from my heart. One of those areas was my expectation of God. Although I'd never said it out loud, even to myself, I believed God couldn't be trusted. The way I saw it, suffering and pain were abundant in the world, and He didn't seem to be doing His part in helping to make things better. God owed me and the rest of the world better than what we were getting. After all, I'd been assaulted at the age of nineteen by a rapist who had attacked more than forty women, and I was a bit slow on the uptake about the idea of forgiving someone I believed I was allowed to justifiably hate—a man who'd raped more than forty women. If he didn't deserve to be hated, then who did?

Of course I didn't articulate my doubts about God out loud. I barely even articulated them to myself. My husband Dan was a Christian school administrator, and I wasn't about to put his career on the line. So instead of investigating my questions, I became the worst kind of Christian—a do-gooder cynic who doesn't confront her own doubt. I put on a mask and became a politically polished critic and a closet skeptic.

But I also became a great server. For all the wrong reasons.

I learned to serve my family, my friends, and my church from the parched recesses of my own need. To fill the growing thirst in my soul, I drank from sources on the surface of life that filled the void inside me—approval of friends and family, public opinion, nods of approval from church culture.

But God has ways of forcing us to look at our false, manufactured images before the mirror of His love. For it's only in His reflection that we can truly see who we are in the image of who He is. It would take me years to understand that truth. But God had time, and He set to work. He wouldn't be content to leave me a *Kum-Bah-Yah* Christian—in name only. He intended to claim me—body, mind, and soul.

Driving the Pipe Deeply:
The Source for the Double-Love Command

As caregivers, we're all thirsty. We all know at our core that our resources are limited, and suffering at times can seem to know no bounds. We're all searching for an *actual* source from which to draw purpose and meaning for a journey into pain and sorrow.

Our most critical realization as caregivers must be that our highest priority can never be the giving of care or even the sacrificial pouring out of our lives. While these loving motives may be rooted deeply in our hearts, *doing* tasks and *performing* services must never define the core of our being. Our sustenance for caregiving must ebb from a source that runs deep within us, and our doing for others must well up from the overflow from that source. Unless our sustaining source in all of life is God himself, the Source of All That Is Actual, we will eventually become mired in self-service, discouragement, and depression.

The highest priority for the caregiver must be one thing and one thing alone—to become totally and completely immersed in the wellspring of God—for out of our intimate relationship with God will flow the enablement to be all we were meant to be in Christ, and out of that abundance we will find the source for all we will ever need as caregivers.

Scripture tells us that God longs to know us in heart-to-heart intimacy, to hear our confidences, our longings, our heart cries. Like young lovers who live for the next conversation with their beloved, we should be so reliant upon moment-by-moment communication with God that we can't survive an hour without sharing our hearts with Him. This is ultimately what will sustain us in our journey.

God longs to know us relationally. He doesn't care how much we know about Him, how much we talk about Him, or how many sermons we've heard about Him. He longs to grab us in His arms, draw us close, and stare into our eyes. In his book entitled *Divine Embrace*, Ken Gire shares, "Maybe it's not so much lessons in dancing we need as lessons in loving, because the Christian life is about intimacy, not technique. The Lord of the dance doesn't want us worrying about our feet. He doesn't want us worrying about the steps ahead. He simply wants us to feel the music, fall into his arms, and follow his lead."[1]

The love relationships portrayed between God and His people and Christ and His beloved as seen throughout Scripture are deeply intimate: a bride beloved by her groom, a shepherd bearing his lost sheep. God longs for us to know His passion for us and to respond to Him in an outpouring of love. What He desires most is for us to see His limitless love for us and to be moved.

This explains why Jesus' response to the Pharisees during the final week of His earthly ministry was so critically important. In Matthew 22:37–39, the Pharisees approached Jesus with a question: "What is the most important commandment? Their question, of course, was a total sham. They had no desire to know Jesus' heart or to keep His teaching. But His response encapsulated His passion and the culmination of His earthly ministry: " 'Love the Lord your God with all your heart and with all your soul and with all

---

1. Ken Gire, *Divine Embrace* (Wheaton, Illinois: Tyndale House Publishers, 2003), 7.

your mind.' This is the first and greatest commandment. And the second is like it: 'Love your neighbor as yourself.'"

Love God with your heart first, and the soul and mind will follow.

The next statement is startling. We are to love our neighbor with the same priority that we love God and that we love ourselves—with all our heart, soul, and mind. Jesus knew that our love for others would come from the natural outflow of our love for Him.

This double-love command became the challenge of humanity from the moment of Eve's conversation with the serpent in the Garden of Eden. Will you love God and trust His character or not? And it's our challenge every day because it is a challenge of priorities that find their

> "Maybe it's not so much lessons in dancing we need as lessons in loving, because the Christian life is about intimacy, not technique. The Lord of the dance doesn't want us worrying about our feet. He doesn't want us worrying about the steps ahead. He simply wants us to feel the music, fall into his arms, and follow his lead."
>
> KEN GIRE, *Divine Embrace*

fountainhead in the heart. Proverbs 27:19 states, "As water reflects a face, so a man's heart reflects the man."

God's first priority is reflected in the double-love command: His desire is to capture our hearts. Our hearts are the source of our image-bearing—an image that overshadows every moment of our lives and that will either lift us up or drag us below in the day-to-day challenges of our caregiving.

When all is stripped away, God longs for us to love Him for who He is, apart from what He gives us, apart from what He provides for us, apart from anything we can see or measure for ourselves.

Even when the world doesn't make sense.

Even in the midst of pain.

Even when we're suffering, or those we love most are suffering.

Why? Because we can trust in the character of a sovereign God who wove together the fabric of eternity, the timelines of history, and the love of a Father just to redeem us. This is the wellspring that runs deep beneath the circumstances of life and enables us to serve, to love, to care, to forgive, and to hope in the midst of suffering and pain.

When Jesus encapsulated the passion and purpose of His life in response to the Pharisees—to those who despised Him and sought to pervert His every good intent for the world—He couldn't have been any clearer.

Let love for God overwhelm your heart. Let it engulf the center of your being. Let it so captivate you that it possesses your emotions, your mind, and your actions. And when you do, your life will pour out in service to others as you take on the nature of Christ through the power of the Holy Spirit.

> "Jesus Christ by His redemption can make our actual lives in keeping with our religious professions … The principles of Jesus … soak right down to our very makeup … God remakes us, puts His Holy Spirit in us, then the Holy Spirit applies the same principles to us and enables us to work them out by His guidance."
>
> OSWALD CHAMBERS,
> "God's Character and the Believer's Conduct," Studies in the Sermon on the Mount.

And will your efforts ever fall short? For many of us, much of the time.

Will we struggle against the temptation to pour out our care-giving from the muddied waters of our emotional reserves? Yes.

Will we attempt to squeeze out a few more drops of our own wisdom for the tough questions? Sometimes.

Will we muster up our own sheer determination to simply get through the next task, through the next day? Perhaps.

In her New York Times best-selling book Another Country, internationally noted psychologist and author Dr. Mary Pipher states,

People want things to go well, but they are human. There is baggage from the past, as well as trouble in the present. Our parents weren't perfect parents, and we weren't perfect children. Nobody becomes a perfect person with age. Even when everyone wants things to end on a good note, problems come up. How could they not in such difficult and unknown territory? Loving people means being disappointed.[2]

My pastor has taught me the truth that the big picture always interprets the little picture. Eternity always interprets what we see today. We can rest in the fact that God's grace and God's character never change. The wellsprings of supply are always there, always available. But when we seek to love others and meet their needs from our limited resources or when we seek to love God first with our limited emotions or intellect, we will always fall short. It is only when we root our understanding and worship deeply in His character that loving Him with our soul and mind and loving others can be possible. To do it in reverse order is a matter of the will and will collapse in failure.

> "The big picture always interprets the little picture. Eternity always interprets what we see today."
>
> PASTOR LOUIE KONOPKA

Farewell to Kum-Bah-Yah: First Glimpses in the Mirror of God's Grace

The message was simple the Sunday morning I first fell in love with Jesus. It was the morning I was swept away in the overwhelming awareness of my sins and the fact that I stood at the foot of the cross shoulder-to-shoulder beside the rapist who had attacked me, awash in the same outpouring of God's love. It was the morning I became truly aware of the magnitude of God's love for me.

---

2. Mary Pipher, *Another Country: Navigating the Emotional Terrain of Our Elders* (New York: Riverhead Books, 1999), 123–124.

Over the years, I would struggle to serve and care for others from the source of the *Actual* that I found that day. But it would be my starting point, as over and over again God would bring me back to my sufficiency in Him.

Drawing from the Depths: The Character of God

As caregivers, we often look for the resources for our daily challenges in the pools and streams of encouragement that lie upon the surface of our lives. Yet true sustenance lies deep beneath the surface in the *Actual*—in the character of God himself.

In his book *God: As He Longs for You to See Him,* author and pastor Chip Ingram comments on the words of A. W. Tozer: "What comes into our minds when we think about God is the most important thing about us... The most portentous fact about any man is not what he at any given time may say or do, but what he in his deep heart conceives God to be like."[3]

As caregivers, we often seek to find our supply for carrying out our daily tasks in the pools and streams of encouragement that lie upon the surface of our lives. Yet our sustenance lies deep beneath the surface in the actual—the character of God himself.

Our perceptions of God will control our hearts, our motives, our goals, and our success or failure in living out the double-love command. And if, at the core of our being, we do not trust in the character of God first and foremost, we will draw our strength from our circumstances, from the encouragement and ministry of others, from the sermons and devotionals we hear. But if at the center of our being we have not found utter rest, utter devotion, utter trust in the character of our loving and sovereign heavenly Father, we will be drawing from the surfaces of spirituality.

3. A. W. Tozer, *Knowledge of the Holy*, as quoted in Chip Ingram, *God: As He Longs for You to See Him* (Grand Rapids, Michigan: Baker Books, 2004), 31.

God desires for our rest to be found in Him alone, in our quiet confidence in His innate nature. In Psalm 46:10, the psalmist reflects his deep trust in the character of God: "Be still and know that I am God." Psalm 112:7 echoes the same quiet assurance: "He will have no fear of bad news; his heart is steadfast, trusting in the Lord."

As caregivers, we daily face the tough questions, the harsh realities, the heart-rending uncertainties. It is only as we gaze into the eyes of our loving God, fall into His embrace, and give way to His next steps that we will gain strength for the journey.

Roadside Assistance

See appendix 3, "Tips for Assessing and Addressing Caregiver Burnout."

Guzzling from the Pipe:
Our Source of Strength in the *Actual* God

I've spent a good portion of my life searching for a Victorian garden and rummaging through my cluttered and dusty spiritual cupboards for an artsy urn when all along there was an *actual* artesian well outside my door, and God was asking me to bring only myself and a thirst for Him. The water was there—a steady stream—pure and sweet. God was waiting for me to run to it, with all the abandon of a child who clamps his mouth over the water hose on a hot summer day.

Come and drink and never thirst again. I have empowered you with everything for life and godliness and have given you the same Holy Spirit I poured out over my Son.

And as certainly as the sun rises every morning, God waits for me to run to Him and collapse at His feet just so we can nestle together and chat. And as I learn to love Him, my love for others will gush forth as a byproduct of my love for Him. I won't be able to help myself.

God knows that as I give Him my heart, my emotions, my will, and my actions will follow. I will begin to love my neighbor as myself. Loving God will pour out of me into the way I love people. It will be impossible to say that I love God and not love people as I love myself. As I love God more, living the double-love command will become a lifestyle. I myself will become the *actual* person God intended me to be, more fully loving those God entrusts into my care, becoming the true caregiver God intended me to be.

Until I, too, like Mona and Louie, become motivated to give more than I ever receive.

Praise God, from whom all blessings flow.

Prayer

Father God, stir in me a longing to know you deeply, intimately. Forgive me for the sin of judging you according to my own small and distorted ideas of who you should be. Enlarge my heart. Multiply my capacity to love you and to know your love—to understand the amazing promise that you love me with an everlasting love. May my thirst for you grow stronger each day, and may I learn what it means to live in intimate communication with you as I walk through each day in prayer. May I learn to love and serve out of the overflow of my love for you and to more deeply and fully come to reflect your image to others. Amen.

Meditation and Personal Application Questions

1. In what ways do you think an understanding of the double-love command and the character of God may have impacted Mona and Louie's caregiving? What do you see in their story that influenced your opinion?

2. What are the central perceptions that you hold regarding the character of God? Do you regard Him as fully, purely trustworthy, in spite of circumstances? Do you feel you have to earn His approval? Do you feel He would love you more if you were doing things differently? Are your opinions of God's character rooted in Scripture or in your subjective feelings and experiences?

3. How does your love for God impact your love for others and the way you carry out the double-love command in your everyday life? Do you feel you struggle in loving others as yourself? In what ways?

4. Where have you struggled most with loving God with all your heart? Do you feel He has been unjust? Unmerciful? Unloving? Do you feel He is trustworthy? Do you struggle with anger at God? Have you explored these areas of your heart and sought biblical counsel?

Scripture for Further Meditation

God's holiness:	Exodus 15:11
God's love:	Isaiah 54:10
God the creator:	Nehemiah 9:6
God's sovereignty:	Psalm 93:1–2

Resources on the Character of God

Chip Ingram, *God As He Longs for You to See Him* (Baker Book House, 2004).

Oswald Chambers, *Studies in the Sermon on the Mount: God's Character and the Believer's Conduct* (Discovery House Publishers, 1995).

"Arise, my darling, my beautiful one, and come with me.
See! The winter is past; the rains are over and gone.
Flowers appear on the earth; the season of singing has come,
the cooing of doves is heard in our land.
The fig tree forms its early fruit;
the blossoming vines spread their fragrance.
Arise, come, my darling; my beautiful one, come with me."

SONG OF SONGS 2:10–12

Chapter Three

A Man Named Fred and the Power of Story

Seeing Your Loved One through New Eyes

"From the time I was young, I never understood my dad. Everything in his life seemed to be driven by duty. It was as if he felt it was wrong to do anything for enjoyment or for himself. He never had a hobby other than Bible reading, and it seemed like he felt it was sinful to draw pleasure from life.

"When I was in college my mom told me that when my father was ten years old, he'd helped his brothers cut his father down from the barn where he'd committed suicide. It was during the Depression. He was the second oldest son in a family of five. As I grew older, I learned bits and pieces of the family story—how his father had struggled with depression, how each of the boys had been shaped in one way or another by that day.

"In my father's final years, when he struggled with severe anxiety and mental illness, knowing his childhood story helped me understand to some extent the mental anguish he was suffering. It gave me compassion I don't think I would have had, had I not been able to see that, as long as he lived, somewhere inside of him was a broken child, weeping for his father."

Dan

⌒

*W*e wear glimpses of our life stories in our eyes. I saw Fred's in the first moment I met him.

A man whose seventy or so years were etched deeply into his face, he blew through the front door of the bookstore as if he owned the place, stopping short at my signing table as he quickly flipped through the pages of my newly published Christian novel. The disdain rose on his face, and he slammed the book back down.

"I'd never buy this. Wouldn't read it if you gave it to me. Did the religion thing once and it didn't get me anything in the end."

I was sure he would head to the back of the store, far from the likes of me. But instead, he settled into a chair near mine in a nook where I had been tucked away out of the flow of heavy traffic coming through the door. In spite of his irritation, something told me I would know a lot about Fred before the next two hours had ended. I hoped he would know a lot about me.

"What's your story about anyway?" He glanced up from his newspaper. He was the kind of man whose internal timer compelled him to speak every few seconds. I knew we would get along fine.

I smiled. "My book's about my life, but through the eyes of other characters. It's about whether God's a monster who can't control the world He created. It's about a teenage girl who accidentally drowns her little sister."

An expletive flew from his lips, and he returned to his newspaper. A minute later the second question came.

"Why would a nice 'Christian' lady like you want to write about garbage like that? Don't you Christians just try to explain away the suffering in the world anyway?"

I chose the sliver of my story his eyes had told me he and I would share. "I had to figure out for myself if God was a monster. You're right—there's suffering in the world. A man who had raped forty women attacked me in my own bed. A few years later someone my husband and I trusted molested our daughter. So I wasn't so sure I wanted to trust God if He said He loved me but was willing to let me and my children suffer."

Fred folded his newspaper slowly and laid it aside. Then he reached out and picked up one of my books and began to thumb through. I watched his eyes as my story mingled with his—the suffering and pain, the doubts that had dragged him under.

Over the next two hours I listened to Fred as more questions came, more expletives, more silences as he scanned the pages of my book. Then fragments of his story attached to mine, and he slowly saw bits and pieces of himself in my eyes. He told me of the pain of rejection, of divorce, of a broken family, of guilt and remorse.

Before I left that day Fred's story and mine had intertwined. He purchased my novel, and he asked when I would be back so he could buy my next book. He asked about my children, my husband, my parents, my faith.

My story unleashed his and broke down walls of separation.

You and I are a lot alike, Fred. I know what it feels like to lose hope, and I see where hope in God can take you.

In the flickering moments where my story converged with Fred's, hope was born in his heart in a dance of grace.

⸻

The power of story is the power of transformation. As Bayard Taylor, author and worldview authority states, "Each moment of a story is like a moment in our lives, a little part of our larger story, one that we're constantly interpreting and replaying."[1] And those stories that resonate most deeply in our hearts are those that expose our struggles against who we are and what we cannot overcome on our own.

As we interact with those around us, God offers us the opportunity to be transformed as we find points of connection between our stories and theirs.

God's redemption story is the story of eternity touching temporality, as we are overcome by His love, ambushed by His grace, and transformed by His transcendence. The redemption story is God's story intertwined with ours, bringing purpose and meaning where there was none.

---

1. Bayard Taylor, "Big Story, Your Part," *Focus on the Family*, June 2007, 12.

It is this redemptive, image-bearing power that we are privileged to reflect in our caregiving—the power to pour out grace and partner with God in changing the course of eternity as we mingle our life with the life of another.

If we will just open our hearts to the moments.

A Road Map for the Journey: The Stories of Life

In his book *Epic*, John Eldredge shares that stories are the road maps of our lives, the way we figure things out. "Bring two people together and they will soon be telling stories. A child on her grandmother's lap. Two men in a fishing boat. Strangers stuck another hour in an airport. Simply run into a friend. What do you want to know?"[2] Stories help us see a beginning, middle, and an end. They help us see the motivations, purposes, and goals behind people's actions and in life itself. Without story, life itself has no meaning. It becomes "a tale told by an idiot, full of sound and fury."[3]

Roadside Assistance

See appendices 7 and 8 at the back of the book for ideas on how to share your stories with your elderly loved ones, as well as tips on communicating more effectively with the elderly.

Jesus used the power of story throughout His ministry, and He often used parables as He taught the crowds. Matthew 13:34 tells us, "Jesus spoke all these things to the crowd in parables; he did not say anything to them without using a parable." Jesus knew the power of story to create intimacy, to evoke empathy, and, ultimately, to engage the heart. And the heart was, after all, where He chose to make His home. Yet he also used the power of parables to

---

2. John Eldredge, *Epic: The Story God Is Telling and the Role That Is Yours to Play* (Nashville, Tennessee: Thomas Nelson Publishers, 2004), 4.

3. William Shakespeare, *Macbeth*, act 5, scene 2, lines 26–28.

hide truth from His listeners, obscuring the spiritual from the eyes of non-discerning hearts (Matthew 13:11).

Stories of the Heart:
Embarking on the Road to Understanding

As caregivers, we often view our roles as *doers*, performing acts of service for those we minister to. But that is only an embarkation point for our journey. As we provide care for others, God intends for our lives to *converge*, and convergence comes at the touch points of the heart.

Jesus' goal wasn't to receive an act of service from the woman at the well—He orchestrated a life-upon-life convergence that would eternally change her heart. His words and actions told her that He knew her story, that He empathized with her, that He cared about the totality of her heart and life. Jesus' connection with her in those brief moments told her immediately of His compassion. The look in His eyes, the touch of His hand, the tone of His voice communicated as clearly as His words. She walked away that day forever changed because Jesus walked into her story with a commitment to rewriting the ending.

Jesus' purpose in healing the lame, the lepers, and the blind wasn't simply to restore physical wellness. Moments of shared compassion, intimacy, and revelation—of who He was and of His unfathomable knowledge of who each person He touched was and could become—were moments when the stories of lives were rewritten and penned into eternity. In His role as a caregiver, as in all things, Jesus was also a redeemer.

> Caregiving is perhaps the most redemptive work we will ever do—as we sacrificially pour our lives out on behalf of others.

True caregiving is perhaps the most redemptive work we will ever do—as we sacrificially pour out our lives on behalf of others. It is about touching, seeing, and pouring out as Jesus did.

For no gain or reward.

Despite pain and sorrow.

In the face of sacrifice, with no regard for or repayment or return.

But the trap of caregiving often lies in confusing the path for the journey. Caregiving is simply the road beneath our feet as we journey beside one another. It is not the journey itself. But it is on that path, as our lives converge, that intimacy, empathy, and compassion can take root, and we can grow together.

When Jesus fed the five thousand, His purpose wasn't solely to provide a meal to meet a physical need. His purpose was ultimately to reveal himself and glorify His Father so that people could be transformed into the image bearers God created them to be.

Jesus entered the human story to change our stories, not simply from a temporal perspective, but from an eternal perspective. And as caregivers, where our lives converge with the lives of those we care for, we join God in His plan for the course of eternity. Our vision must extend beyond the physical to the eternal in all that we do.

Across the Time Zones:
Creating Compassion and Connection

The reality of caregiving is that it's messy. Nothing about it proceeds in a straight line from point A to point B. We bring our past roles and relationships, as untidy as they may be, into adulthood with us. Gender roles, sibling relationships, financial expectations, disappointments, grudges, and every heartache ever known to touch the human condition enter into the caregiving equation.

We must expect disappointment and hard work. We must be committed to compassion and heart work.

On a brisk fall day, my husband Dan stood at the edge of a Michigan farm in the shadow of a pristinely painted centennial barn and fulfilled a commitment he had made to himself to enter his father's story in a new way. As he gazed at the barn where his father had played and worked as a child, the man he had struggled so hard to know—the man of long silences, of emotional distances, of surface-level pleasantries—suddenly transformed into a frightened ten-year-old working to cut through the rope tied to the rafters.

A child struggling to carry his dead father back to the house.

A child who struggled to carry the weight of that burden for the rest of his life.

In that moment Dan did not come to know his father perfectly; he simply came to see more clearly how his father came to be the quiet, dutiful man he had always known. That day beside the barn, Dan opened his father's story to a chapter he had never read. He opened himself to compassion, empathy, and connection.

And he never viewed his dad the same way again.

We cannot hope to understand the complexity of one another's stories. But we are asked to work toward creating connection.

You and me are a lot alike, Fred.

Broken.

Needy.

In need of forgiveness and grace.

It's only when we see that truth that we can begin to truly enter one another's stories.

> "We can learn a great deal from the old. They can teach us about the importance of time, relationships and gratitude. They can teach us how to endure and how to be patient. They can help us put our own pains and problems in perspective."
>
> MARY PIPHER, *Another Country: Navigating the Emotional Terrain of Our Elders*

In her New York Times bestseller *Another Country*, Dr. Mary Pipher discusses the concept of time zones in culture—the eras of culture and age that differentiate and shape who we are. She explains how Depression-era adults view life through a different lens from baby boomers, even in things as simple as food. A generation that grew up in poverty may view food as security, whereas a generation that has always had food in abundance might hold a health-conscious attitude toward diet. These "time-zone" gaps can cause conflicts in understanding and communication.

Pipher explains the importance of understanding differences between what something looks like on the surface and what something is truly about. "Thinking in terms of deep structure versus surface structure can help family members understand one another.

Deep structure is about motives. For example, the deep structure of the question 'Do you want some tea?' might be 'I want you to feel welcome in my home.' Different generations share the same deep structure. Everyone wants to give and receive love, to raise healthy children, and to keep things calm and happy. But the surface structure, the words and actions people use to express their motives, can be very different" (p. 70).

> *Roadside Rest*
>
> SCRIPTURE FOR MEDITATION
>
> The purposes of a man's heart are deep waters, but a man of understanding draws them out (Proverbs 20:5).

When we read through Scripture and evaluate the manner in which Jesus interacted with people, it's easy to see that His ultimate goal was always to relate at the deep level, where true connection takes place. This should be our goal as well. As Mary Pipher points out, "Conflicts among surface statements often disappear if deep structures are understood. When people are evaluated in terms of their motives, they are easier to respect and to forgive."[4]

The Simplicity of the Bottom Line:
Motive and Momentum

Our goal in carrying out the double-love command is a simple directive: to love others out of the overflow of our love for God, as His image bearers, and with the same level of priority that we love ourselves.

---

4. *Another Country*, 71.

Devotedly.

Wholeheartedly.

Selflessly.

With every best motive in mind, and without duplicity.

But caregiving can be hard, you say, *the relationships too difficult.*

"I don't want to love my mother," a dear friend told me. But as much as I love my friend, I must remind her that Scripture

is painfully clear. We cannot say we love God and not love our mothers. Or our fathers. Or our children. Or our enemies. But our motive, first and always, must be our unconditional, unequivocal trust in the character of God. Out of that will flow our ability to love others as ourselves.

The rest is a matter of momentum.

A matter of small steps. A matter of obedience to the call.

Perhaps to pray for your loved one.

Perhaps to lay down a simple boundary for the first time—with the grace of Jesus himself, born out of the pure motive of the double-love command.

Perhaps to forgive.

Perhaps to lay down the sword of sarcasm or the maul of martyrdom that you've slung about as your weapons of battle.

Perhaps to give up the reins of control.

Perhaps to take the first tentative steps into someone's story, rather than to stand aloof and rooted in the past.

The ultimate goal of story is redemption through the convergence of lives. To enter the story. To touch a heart. To allow your own heart to be touched.

And in the touching, to be changed.

Physically.

Eternally.

This is the goal of caregiving and of the double-love command: to love God so fully, so completely, that our love for Him envelops the way we see His children—whether lovely or unlovely.

With each new day, we are responsible to fan the flame of God's love in our hearts and let it radiate to our loved ones. And as we are changed, we are empowered to carry the message of hope.

You and I are a lot alike, Fred. More alike than we think.

In the story of our lives, in those moments where compassion and redemption are offered, our lives intertwine in a dance of grace.

And the heavens applaud.

Prayer

Dear Father, I thank you that you chose to invade my story with your own. I thank you that you chose to change my eternal destiny by pouring yourself and your provision into my life. Thank you for the opportunity now to pour that grace into the life of another. Thank you for the joy of joining you in your plan of redemption through joining my life with the life of another. Help me to see my work as a rich gift that will impact the course of eternity and for the blessing of partnering with you to touch lives. Father, give me the grace, wisdom, and provision that I need each day to carry out the tasks that lie ahead. Thank you for the gift of your Holy Spirit, who empowers me each moment of the day.

Meditation and Personal Application Questions

1. In what ways has your story "converged" with the story of someone you're caring for? How do you see this divine convergence reshaping both of your lives? What do you believe God's purposes may be in this?

2. What elements of your loved one's story have been difficult for you to relate to and why? How have "time zone" differences impacted your relationship? Differences in values?

3. In what ways do you see a need to grow in compassion? In empathy? In connection? What small steps of change can you implement to grow in these areas?

4. We may be rebuffed when we reach out. What do these Scripture passages tell us about how we are to respond in the face of rejection: Romans 12:12, 14, 20–21?

5. What areas of self-will and pride cling to the roots of your motives as a caregiver? Do you feel the Holy Spirit convicting you of the need for repentance and, if so, in what specific areas of your life?

Scripture for Further Meditation

Matthew 22:37–39
John 13:34–35
Romans 13:9–10

Resources on Creating Shared Stories

Turn to appendix 7 for a list of suggested topics for sharing stories cross-generationally. This list is intended to be an idea generator for your own creativity.

Several years ago one family decided they would use family reunions to record the memories of aging relatives. Each year they choose a specific era or event for family members to reminisce about, and their interactions are videotaped for their family archives.

Another popular idea has been to create family blogs. The technologically savvy generation can be made responsible for updating and creating the material periodically, but it's a great way to keep family members informed about each other and to pass information, current or past, about one another.

Therefore, as God's chosen people, holy and dearly loved,
clothe yourselves with compassion, kindness, humility,
gentleness and patience.
Bear with each other and forgive whatever grievances you may
have against one another. Forgive as the Lord forgave you.
And over all these virtues put on love,
which binds them all together in perfect unity.

COLOSSIANS 3:12-14

Chapter Four

Putting the Samsonite in Satan's Hand

UNLEASHING THE POWER OF FORGIVENESS

"I've been a pastor's wife for over thirty years, and I can't explain the intolerable rage I felt when my mother moved in with me. I've read the books and explored these issues in my life and thought I'd put these things behind me. So why the hair-trigger reactions to things I thought I'd dealt with?

"I deeply resent the way Mom came to live with us. One of my siblings struggles with cancer, and having my mother stay in his home was a disaster. My other brother is fiscally irresponsible and always has been, so that means that, just like when I was a child, I'm picking up the slack for him.

"I want nothing to do with my family right now. I'm angry at them. Mom gave the house to my brother because he's ill. My other brother is financially irresponsible, so I'm stuck with Mom's care, and I'm madder than I've ever been in my life. If you want a story about somebody doing this victoriously, you won't find one here. My childhood and garbage and emotions are flooding out of me right now, and I don't know what to do with them."

Barbara

A middle-aged woman stood near the costume jewelry counter, lumpy and bumpy in a gargantuan plaid jacket stretched over a matronly mid-calf skirt, oblivious to the millions of eyes raking up and down her frumpish girth. As she fingered a double strand of Barbara Bush-esque pearls, two women swooped in on her, one commandeering her from the right, the other from the left. The pearls clattered to the glass countertop as she was spun to face a hidden camera, then visually and verbally dissected before being pronounced dated and dowdy before a growing crowd of passers-by.

Susannah Constantine and Trinny Woodall, hosts of the BBC television show and best-selling book *What Not to Wear*, gave their hapless victim a moment to recover as they introduced another segment of their show to the hidden camera. The two quirky fashion icons, who had gained fame and fortune by ambushing women and revealing their fashion foibles before the eyes of the watching world, had found yet another woman to make over. Her true beauty was there, but hidden beneath layers of polyester and plaid. Susannah and Trinny had the vision to see beneath the surface to what others couldn't see.

This day would become a turning point in the woman's life—the day she learned to see herself as others saw her and found that that was not enough. Little did she know that as the pearls fell from her hand, her life was about to change. Susannah and Trinny were about to transform her from the outside, in.

The premise of the show is transformation. With a few fashion principles and simple design concepts, Susannah and Trinny teach the power to see and to be seen in a new way. The women who stride off camera at the end of their show are the same women who slumped and fled when the camera first rolled. But by the end of the program, their spirits have been sculpted with the hammer and chisel of inner confidence.

And with each ring of the hammer, countenances lift, and a glow begins to radiate from the inside out.

At the end of the show, women walk differently. They talk differently. They see life through a different lens. Not because of fabric and accessories but because they have learned to see themselves with new eyes. They have learned to see themselves through someone else's eyes.

Susannah and Trinny help women transform from the outside, in. They help women see themselves as beautiful and, in seeing, to walk into that reality. Their work begins with the startling revelation of how the world can view the outer disarray we sometimes mindlessly project.

We, too, often walk about, projecting our sinful disarray to a watching world. We, too, are often mindless to the sin that distorts our image to those around us. It's only with the God-given faith and power to see ourselves as God sees us that we, too, will have the power to be transformed by the Holy Spirit. And it is only as we develop the power to see the sin that distorts both our inner and our outer images that we will have the ability to truly forgive.

The Power to See: The Power to Forgive

Take a look at most families, and you'll find plenty of reasons to exercise forgiveness.

The truth of the matter is that even well-meaning parents, siblings, children, and extended family members manage to offend, insult, ignore, suffocate, exaggerate, defend, isolate, withdraw, obsess, rationalize, deny, polarize, and act out a host of other prickly verbs we could place on a list. Even more disturbing is the fact that sometimes downright nasty parents, siblings, children, and extended family members often manage to maim, sack, and pillage their way through life, leaving the ravages of destruction for others to piece together.

And as caregivers, we're often stuck in the middle. On a recent call-in talk show, a

> Forgiveness does not mean ignoring what has been done or putting a false label on an evil act. It means, rather, that the evil act no longer remains a barrier to the relationship.
> MARTIN LUTHER KING, JR.

Roadside Assistance

How do we let go of the past? Here are five steps to forgiveness:

- Instead of trying to convince yourself that you don't care, acknowledge the pain you have suffered.
- Get information. Find out how the person who hurt you got to be who he or she is.
- Be willing to turn that information into understanding of the person who hurt you.
- Make a conscious choice to let understanding lead to forgiveness.
- Set boundaries. Do not continue to accept hurtful behaviors.

Grace Kettering, MD and Kathy King, PhD, *Real Solutions for Caring for Your Elderly Parent*, 102-103

---

woman asked me a difficult question that portrays the complexity of the issues many caregivers face:

> My father has Alzheimer's, and my family members believe I'm the daughter who should take Dad into her home and care for him during these next years. But no one knows that when I was a child my dad repeatedly molested me. What am I supposed to do?

It was a question that gave me pause—for many reasons. For her pain. For her isolation. For her father's pain. For his isolation. For the trauma and tragedy of sin.

But also for the triumph we can claim over sin and for the comfort we can claim in our pain and isolation. Often our greatest triumph is seeing our own sin clearly enough to be willing to lay our bitterness and anger at the foot of the cross and to see those who have hurt us through Jesus' eyes. Perhaps it's because I'm such a slow learner that I could feel this woman's struggle.

We're all rebellious sinners, broken by bitterness, perverted by pride. Lumpy, bumpy, caricatures of who God created us to be, taken in by the allure of fake pearls.

Until God spins us away from our sin-centered reflections to face Him and to show us who we really are.

The beautiful children He created us to be. His chosen ones. Holy. Dearly beloved. With the power to forgive as we've been forgiven.

God's Glad Rags: Unleashing the Power

Possessing the clarity of vision to see ourselves as God sees us is the bedrock of our power to forgive. Our willingness and ability to forgive reflects our image-bearing at its deepest level. Forgiveness assumes that we see beyond ourselves and beyond our needs to the greater good, to the eternal picture. True forgiveness assumes that we have willingly taken on the yoke of bearing the grievances and offenses of others as Christ did—willingly and humbly.

Colossians 3:12–14 shows us the wardrobe of transformation. These garments of holiness make it possible for us to forgive.

> The worldly man treats people kindly because he "likes" them: the Christian, trying to treat everyone kindly, finds himself liking more and more people as time goes on—and people he could not even have imagined himself liking at the beginning.
>
> C. S. Lewis,
> *Mere Christianity*

- **Compassion**. Charles Spurgeon said, "There are none so tender as those who have been skinned themselves." Our compassion is rooted in our knowledge of *who we are*—joint heirs with Christ. Our compassion is not rooted in how others regard us or how we are treated. It is a reflection of our character in Christ. As we forgive, we take on God's perspective and character, and our capacity for compassion and understanding of compassion grow.

- **Kindness.** C. S. Lewis summarized the transformation principle well: "The worldly man treats people kindly because he 'likes' them: the Christian, trying to treat everyone kindly, finds himself liking more and more people as time goes on—and people he could not even have imagined himself liking at the beginning." Kindness should drape all God's children like a well-worn cloak.

- **Humility.** Spencer W. Kimball has said that humility is "greatness in plain clothes." True garments of humility are worn out at the knees from kneeling in prayer and from time spent in service to others. The humble know that their confidence lies in who they are in Christ—not who they are in the eyes of men.

- **Gentleness.** "There is nothing stronger in the world than gentleness." These words from Mother Teresa depict the power of the simple, for her life shone with the transforming power of gentleness. Her sacrificial ministration poured out in service to others is a model of caregiving.

- **Patience.** Leonardo da Vinci summed up the power of patience to transform our character: "Patience serves as a protection against wrongs as clothes do against cold. For if you put on more clothes as the cold increases, it will have no power to hurt you. So in like manner you must grow in patience when you meet with great wrongs, and they will be powerless to vex your mind."

- **Love.** Surpassing all we understand, encompassing all we are, compelling all we do is our motive of love, love for the Father that springs from the overwhelming awareness of what we have been forgiven. H. L. Mencken has said, "Love cures people, both the ones who give it and the ones who receive it." Love for others, rooted in our faith in the goodness of God and our commitment to the double-love command, will transform not only those around us but will transform us—from the outside in—as we pour out compassion, kindness, humility, gentleness, and patience on those around us.

The Painful View from the 360-Degree Mirror: Measuring Up

Cami and Darice, the precious caregivers who assisted us in our home, usually made their daily appearance on alternating mornings at about eight a.m. It was always my goal to be clothed before they arrived in order to appear organized and dignified, but I typically hit that goal only once every third week, on days beginning with the letter R. But these dear ladies became family and accepted me in even my most frightening morning disarray. But in spite of their love and acceptance, I wouldn't have thought for a moment of climbing into my minivan in my comfy gray robe to head out to conduct the day's business.

Early on in life, I learned to change my clothes every day. Not only that, my mother taught me to put on *clean* clothes—something I worked hard to reinforce with my children in their early years. Somehow, without clean clothes, I just can't start my day with that "fresh as a daisy" feeling.

Forgiveness for everyone—caregivers or care receivers; parents or children; brothers or sisters; those who are married, divorced, separated, widowed, or single—must become a lifestyle issue. "Clothing" and "putting on" are daily acts. Forgiveness is a daily act. And if we place ourselves in the 360-degree mirror of Colossians 3:12–14, we can see how we measure up.

Therefore, as God's chosen people, holy and dearly loved, clothe yourselves with compassion, kindness, humility, gentleness and patience. Bear with each other and forgive whatever grievances you may have against one another. Forgive as the Lord forgave you. And over all these virtues put on love, which binds them all together in perfect unity (Colossians 3:12–14).

Contrasting Views

Compassion	Indifference
Is my heart stirred by spiritual and daily life concerns for this person? Am I able to see this person through Christ's eyes?	Do I prefer to avoid this person and entanglement in her life? Do I see this person in part or largely through my own pain, wounding, or judgmental attitude?
Kindness	**Tolerance**
Do I perform simple acts of kindness for this person with joy? Is my motive for my actions to truly serve out of love and to glorify God?	Do I feel like a martyr when I do things for this person? Is my motive for my actions to do something I've been "trapped" into doing?
Humility	**Judgmentalism**
Am I content to let God be responsible for changing this person? Do I see myself as giving to this person out of the abundance of what God has given to me?	Do I try to force change on this person? Do I see myself giving to this person because God requires me to, even though I believe he or she really doesn't deserve it?
Gentleness	**Harshness**
Does your tone communicate affirmation? Do your body language and attitude communicate affirmation?	Does your tone communicate annoyance, ridicule, condescension? Do your body language and attitude communicate annoyance, ridicule, condescension?

Patience	Annoyance
Do you truly listen and give of yourself? Do you give when it's painful and costs you something?	Do you refuse to emotionally invest in this person? Do you find yourself easily irritated with this person and willing to share your irritation with others?
Love	Self-Service
Do you see yourself standing among the vilest of sinners at the foot of cross, in need of the same forgiveness? Do you pour out your love on others freely and without regard for ever receiving anything in return?	Do you see yourself as somehow different from the person you're called to forgive—less in need of God's forgiveness than she is? Are your acts of kindness a duty, an obligation, a way to win approval, a way to be seen by others?

Coming to Grips with the Lumps and Bumps: It's All in the Name

We all walk about showing a few lumps and bumps to the world, no matter how hard we struggle to hide them. Some of us have corseted ourselves so tightly with unforgiveness that we can draw only the shallowest of spiritual breaths. Our woundedness, bitterness, and lack of joy prevent us from inhaling the beauty and blessings God intended us to enjoy.

In God's 360-degree mirror of truth, the answer to one question tells us a lot about ourselves.

Who do you struggle most to forgive?

For most of us, one name will spring immediately to mind, perhaps two. For many caregivers, that person is a father or mother under their care or perhaps a sibling refusing to help.

And whether we realize it, the lumps and bumps of our relationship with that person hang on our frame like a cheap polyester suit for the entire world to see.

My part in forgiveness:	God's part in forgiveness:
Showing compassion, kindness, humility, gentleness, and patience. Bearing with grievances. Putting on love, ministering to spiritual and practical needs. Committing to act always with the other's best interests in mind (actions, thoughts, tongue, intents).	Changing the heart, mind, and actions of the person I'm responsible for forgiving. Convicting of sin. Meeting spiritual needs for love, pardon, and acceptance. Working out the details of inequity in a fallen and sinful world.

Trying It On, Making It Ours: Steps to Forgiveness

So as caregivers, who are we asked to forgive?

Distracted doctors.

Stubborn siblings.

Selfish spouses.

Callous children.

We're asked to forgive the offenses of our childhood, the offenses of last week, and the offenses that occurred an hour ago when we hung up the phone.

We're asked to forgive on a daily basis, often an hourly basis, and walk out repentance and forgiveness as a lifestyle, because the two go hand-in-hand.

I cannot forgive until I first see that my unwillingness to forgive offends God's character so deeply that the forgiveness He directs toward me is contingent upon the forgiveness I pour out upon others. Scripture makes it clear that while God's love is unconditional, His forgiveness is not. We can block God's willingness to forgive us with our own hardened attitudes.

Matthew 18:21–35 makes it clear that God's forgiveness for us is in direct relationship to our willingness to forgive our brother from our heart (v. 35). Our unforgiving spirits can actually cut off our intimacy with God and block His blessing in our lives. This is best understood when we grasp the truth that, apart from God's total, unconditional, unfathomable forgiveness for us, we are but dust. Unforgiveness is our way of cheapening God's greatest gift to us and hoarding it in selfish ingratitude.

Roadside Rest

SCRIPTURE FOR MEDITATION

For if you forgive men when they sin against you, your heavenly Father will also forgive you. But if you do not forgive men their sins, your Father will not forgive your sins (Matthew 6:14–15).

To love means to forgive even in those moments when we do not get what we believe we deserve. This truth is the essence of the cross, and it is both our calling and our privilege. To believe less and to live less is to defraud God.

Slipping into New Clothes: Steps to Forgiveness

So how do we do this when hurtful actions against us are sometimes ongoing, when the perpetrator is unremorseful, when the situation seems beyond hope?

- Recognize that forgiveness is hard, but it's the only path to freedom. Forgiveness frees us to be the person God intended us to be. Secondly, it frees us from bondage to the person we've been unable to forgive.
- Recognize that the foundation for forgiveness is gratitude for God's abundant mercy. Forgiveness begins with looking at ourselves first, with a commitment to confession and repentance as a lifestyle. As a lifestyle, forgiveness involves a daily "putting on" and "taking off" of sinful attitudes and

worldly rationalizations, self-centered desires, and distorted motives.

- Recognize that forgiveness means laying down what someone else may owe us and never picking it up again.
- Recognize that forgiveness does not mean an abandonment of healthy, biblical boundaries. Forgiveness does not mean allowing people to abuse us. Instead, it allows us to make healthy, responsible choices.
- Recognize that forgiveness does not deny wrong actions against us or deny us the opportunity to grieve what has hurt us. Acknowledge the pain and hurt; tell God how you feel; grieve the loss. Understand that hurt may last for a long time, but that as you gain God's perspective, your perspective will change.
- Make a choice to forgive every aspect of whatever offenses God brings to mind, leaving judgment to God while you pray for the Holy Spirit's healing.
- Recognize that forgiveness does not mean attempting to divert the consequences of sin for those who have sinned against us. The consequences of sin are often intended to be God's spiritual training ground in the lives of those who have made bad choices with long-term implications.
- Recognize that as a lifestyle, forgiveness is a day-by-day experience.

Ephesians 4:31–32 explains the steps to forgiveness, a process of "putting off" and "taking on."

> Get rid of all bitterness, rage and anger, brawling and slander, along with every form of malice. Be kind and compassionate to one another, forgiving each other, just as in Christ God forgave you.

The steps are simple. First, acknowledge our anger and substitute love. Second, reject bitterness—strip it off and toss it aside—

and substitute compassion. Third, put away the desire to stir up dissension, to talk and gossip, to foster thoughts of revenge and even the score, and substitute kindness, gentleness, and tenderness. And finally, forgive each other as Christ forgave us.

God's simple plan for forgiveness, to be walked out in the day-to-day struggle of real-life relationships and real-life pain. And the day we take the first step to strip off the filthy garments of unforgiveness and resentment we've worn so long will be the day our own transformation begins.

The Pearls in Your Hand:
The Clatter of Sinful Pride

Perhaps the greatest struggle for caregivers is the struggle against martyrdom—the nagging voice that we're being asked to do what others don't have to do or won't do. The still, small voice that whispers that we're being abused or taken advantage of. The voice that tells us that we're missing out on something and we're entitled to at least a little resentment. At those who aren't carrying their weight. At parents who didn't prepare and left us holding the bag. At siblings who don't have time to pick up the phone or offer to take Mom or Dad for the weekend. At friends who don't call any more. At the parent we nursed in our home for six years who gave her entire estate to our brother.

We may find the easiest trap is to look around us and find so many to forgive, without looking inward to our own roots of bitterness and pride.

God's greatest gift to us is change. It is why He doesn't leave us standing at the cosmetic counter with costume jewelry hanging from our fingers. He loves us enough to spin us before a watching world and expose our lumps and bumps.

So that He can transform us more into the chosen, holy, and dearly loved children He created us to be.

Prayer

Dear Father, I pray today that you reveal those things to me that I'm oblivious to—those lumps and bumps of sin that distort the person you created me to be. Make me sensitive to the moving of your Holy Spirit in my heart as He stirs in me an awareness of wounds and hurts, bitterness and pride, resentment and rigidity. Dear Father, as these things are revealed to me, I confess them to you as sin and renounce them, asking for your forgiveness and mercy.

Father, give me the power to forgive those who have offended me. Help me to release my expectations of their performing to my standards in return for my forgiveness. Give me discernment in drawing healthy boundaries in my relationship with them—boundaries that challenge me to be all I can be in you and that stir them to godliness motivated by love.

Thank you for your amazing gift of forgiveness poured out in my life that makes it possible for me to forgive others in spite of circumstances. Thank you for the power of your Holy Spirit in my life who continues to convict me of sin and draw me more closely into your loving and outstretched arms.

Meditation and Personal Application Questions

1. Do you believe you live a lifestyle of forgiveness and repentance that reflects your gratitude for what Christ has rescued you from and who He has created you to be in Him?

2. When you hear the question, "Who do you need to forgive?" what name immediately springs to your mind?

3. What small steps of compassion, kindness, humility, gentleness, patience, and love do you believe you're being called to take in regard to this person?

4. Do you fear forgiving? Why? How does your fear line up with the truth of God's Word?

5. What areas in the "Contrasting Views" chart do you struggle with the most? Do you feel the Holy Spirit convicting you in any of these areas? If so, what steps do you believe you need to implement to begin to move toward obedience in these areas? You might want to consider praying over this chart for a few days and asking the Spirit of God to work in your heart in specific areas.

Scripture for Further Meditation

1 John 1:9
Ephesians 1:4–8
Romans 6:17–18, 22–23

Resources

Are you struggling to balance it all? Take time to read and pray over the materials in appendix 3, "Tips on Addressing Caregiver Burnout."

O Lord, you have searched me and you know me.
You know when I sit and when I rise;
you perceive my thoughts from afar.
You discern my going out and my lying down;
you are familiar with all my ways.
Before a word is on my tongue you know it completely,
O Lord... Search me, O God, and know my heart;
test me and know my anxious thoughts.
See if there is any offensive way in me, and lead me
in the way everlasting.

PSALM 139:1-4, 23-24

Chapter Five

Meeting Marie in the Mirror

FACING THE REALITIES OF THE HEART AND THE TONGUE

"I've got to be honest about Rachel's sister. I'm really ticked at her. She lives fifteen minutes from her parents, doesn't have any kids, and she's not willing to help out. Here we are living three hours away with three little kids—one not even old enough to be in school—and Rachel's the one driving down every other weekend to take care of her folks."

Rachel's resignation shows in her voice, and her eyes flicker briefly toward her husband.

"I gave up a long time ago expecting anything out of my sister. She is who she is, and Paul will have to get used to that."

"Yeah. She's a lazy, self-centered whiner."

Rachel sighs. "Tell me how that helps. This is our life. So she doesn't help. It makes me mad, too, but what can I do about it? Nothing. It's what we're stuck with."

Paul and Rachel

⌒

I remember the day I first met Marie Barone—the *other* Marie Barone. I came face to face with her in a moment of self-realization that sucked the breath from my lungs and left me staring at my image in the bathroom mirror for nearly half an hour.

Before that day, I had known Marie only as a sitcom character—the meddling mother-in-law on the television sitcom *Everybody Loves*

Raymond. Marie Barone's life was devoted to self-imposed martyrdom and domestic servitude borne out of a heart of misguided devotion to her married sons and their families. She lived to insinuate her way into the lives of others, using everything from lying to lasagna in order to manipulate and control. Even the simplest compliment from Marie was laced with the cyanide of self-promotion. She was a conniver and a manipulator extraordinaire, but her greatest flaw was her blindness. Marie was incapable of seeing herself as others saw her, of seeing truth and reality in relation to herself. Marie Barone had achieved such a high level of self-deception that any attempt to set her straight was destined to double back and reinforce her warped, idealized image of who she believed herself to be.

One of the most painful days of my life was the day I looked into the mirror and realized that Marie Barone was staring back at me. I had spent almost thirty years molding and shaping a martyr's view of myself and the world around me, and my perspective had become as

Roadside Realities

According to an article by Susan Strecker Richard in *Caring Today* (caringtoday.com), a 2004 Evercare Study of Caregivers in Decline revealed that among 528 caregivers

- 17% report being in fair to poor health, compared to 9% of the general population
- 35% say their health is worse due to caregiving responsibilities
- 75% said that they had no choice in taking their role
- 9% reported being depressed
- 34% provided care an average of 40 hours per week
- The top element that caregivers cited as helping them was personal prayer.

twisted as Marie's. The person I had deceived myself into thinking I was and the person I truly was at the heart level were two entirely different people. And if it hadn't been for the crucible of caregiving, I might never have come to see myself for who I truly was.

I had developed a martyr's heart and tongue. It was ugly. Like a child who had found her mother's lipstick, I'd slathered a bucket-load of spiritual makeup on myself and thought I looked good, without realizing I was parading before the world and my God doing only a clownish imitation of myself.

Until the day I found Marie staring back in the mirror, and something cracked inside my heart. It was the day I crumpled to my knees before God and pleaded for Him to show me my way back to Him and a way out of the life I had created for myself.

Mirror, Mirror, On the Wall: The Truth about Our Motives

The truth of life for all of us is that we struggle with twisted motives, twisted desires, twisted goals, and twisted thinking. At the core of our being, we're selfish creatures, driven by selfish motives.

And caregiving can bring out both the best and the worst in us. If we've ever felt we've had a reason to stand in the center of the universe and scream, "And what about *me?*", it's in our role as a caregiver, where we're asked to lay aside, step aside, suck it up and bind it up and be willing to do it with a smile on our faces and a song in our hearts.

The truth about our motives in even the best of life's circumstances is that we all struggle with a central, sinful desire to promote our own selfish agendas and protect ourselves from being wounded by others. But both of these values run contrary to what the sacrificial life in the trenches is supposed to be for the caregiver.

After living almost thirty years of a life of finely honed martyrdom, I found my caregiving role exposing my false motives and pride like my own personal spiritual Jumbotron. I had been careful to bury my resentment and bitterness beneath a lovely plot of blossoming good works that I had faithfully fertilized with the compost of my amusing sarcasm and blaming spirit. I had learned how to justify my thinking and to make anything and everything anyone else's fault—especially Dan's. And once his father came to live with us, Dan was doomed. On the surface I may have told people that having Norman was a joy, but deep in my heart, I blamed Dan for forcing me into a corner.

I faced a choice. Either I had to take his dad into my home and put on a spiritual face, or I had to do serious business with God and figure out what living out this double-love command was all about.

Ripples in a Warped Reflection

Resentment

Resentment always boils down to one thing: believing we're not getting what we deserve. It means we're telling God and ourselves He doesn't know what He's doing after all and we're entitled to something better. The real struggle for those who are resentful is that their self-justifying attitudes make them blind to the poison in their own hearts.

Martyrdom

Martyrs are looking for someone to notice them—for someone to reflect their feelings about how bad their lives are and to affirm the fact that they're entitled to a bad attitude. Martyrs go a step further than resentment and ask the world to play along in their drama. All the world's a stage for martyrs, as they use their self-justified resentment and their circumstances as megaphones to announce to the world that God isn't good—that He's messed up and given them a raw deal. There's nothing a martyr loves more than another martyr who will reflect back their negative, twisted view of life.

Withdrawal

Withdrawal is often a form of control or opting out. It can be a way of announcing that God gives more than we can bear, and He's often unfair, so we're entitled to bail. When I chose to withdraw, it was usually so Dan would come running to my aid. It was my way of announcing that I wasn't getting enough attention—another weapon in my arsenal of manipulation.

Rationalization

Rationalization in and of itself is not always a bad thing. After all, without rational thinking, we would be subject to the whims of our emotions or the will of others. But when we use rationalization to circumvent truth or righteous choices, no matter how hard they might be, it's always sin. As a caregiver, I found it easy to use rationalization to explain away my manipulative and selfish behavior, when in actuality, my true motives could be twisted and intended to promote my personal agenda. It became easy for me to rationalize that other people *owed* me certain behaviors, attitudes, and actions because of the sacrifices I believed I was making as a caregiver. But when I began making those kinds of rationalizations, I lost the ability to discern the difference between needs and desires, and I became even more manipulative and bitter.

Resignation

Resignation means simply giving up. It means succumbing to mediocrity or less and curling up in a fetal position in the middle of the fight. Resignation is perhaps Satan's most insidious weapon because it is an attack upon our hearts and our passion—upon our commitment to the double-love command itself. Without passion and love, we are nothing.

God makes it abundantly clear that He despises the tepid, the mediocre, the passionless. "I know your deeds, that you are neither cold nor hot. I wish you were either one or the other! So because you are lukewarm—neither hot nor cold—I am about to spit you out of my mouth" (Revelation 3:15–16).

The MARIE Principle:
Facing the Realities of the Heart and the Tongue

Caregiving can be a crucible for spiritual formation. Caregiving reveals our motives, our agendas, our insecurities, our fears, our passions, and our self-will because it strips us down and asks us to place the welfare of others before our own. As caregivers we're often asked to lay a great deal on the altar—our privacy, our homes, our time, our relationships, our financial choices, our job security, our retirement, and our futures—all for what the world might define as a diminishing return or no return at all.

In the world's eyes, and even in the eyes of many believers, caregiving can be a circumstance of life where we're forced to throw up our hands, sigh, and simply put on our best church face. We may

Roadside Assistance

"Forgive family members who choose not to get involved in a loved one's care. It may not be easy; you may feel angry or resentful because the rest of the family isn't doing as much as you are . . . To free yourself from them, try thinking about all that you'll gain from giving care. You'll have a chance to reassess your priorities and decide what really matters in your life."

BETH WITROGEN MCLEOD, ED.,
And Thou Shalt Honor: The Caregiver's Companion

feel we're entitled to a little resentment, a little martyrdom, a little withdrawal, a little rationalization, and a little resignation.

But that's where the Word of God reflects a different truth.

> And whatever you do, whether in word or deed, do it all in the name of the Lord Jesus, giving thanks to God the Father through him (Colossians 3:17).

> Rejoice in the Lord always. I will say it again: Rejoice! Let your gentleness be evident to all. The Lord is near (Philippians 4:4–5).

> I know what it is to be in need, and I know what it is to have plenty. I have learned the secret of being content in any and every situation, whether well fed or hungry, whether living in plenty or in want. I can do everything through him who gives me strength (Philippians 4:12–13).

> Consider it pure joy, my brothers, whenever you face trials of many kinds, because you know that the testing of your faith develops perseverance (James 1:2).

As believers, we're held to a higher standard—the standard of the double-love command: to trust in the character of God in all things, to love Him devotedly, and to love others from the overflow of that love. And as we live out the double-love command, we will be empowered to walk out five simple steps of the MARIE Principle that will transform our caregiving focus, our hearts, and our tongues.

Magnify God

Recognize God's character and goodness in our lives. Praise Him for who He is and all He has done—not just the things we can see, but the things that go beyond our earthly perception.

Consciously practice the power of praise in our lives, both personally and publicly. Choose to focus our thoughts and our tongues on the inexhaustible goodness of God. Praise is the taproot to the power of God in our lives.

When we complain and grumble, we're ultimately saying that God is not good, that He's given us a raw deal, and that we deserve better. Magnifying God acknowledges His sovereign lordship and affirms in our minds and before a watching world that in spite of the difficulties of life, we trust in a good and loving heavenly Father who graciously oversees every detail of life.

Appreciate Others

When my children were small, they had a toy called the See 'n Say, a toy that should become a model for my life. The toy features a dial with pictures of things that make recognizable sounds and a string attached to its side. When you point the arrow on the dial at the picture of a cow, for example, and pull the string, the toy says, "The cow says moo." As a caregiver, I need to learn to develop a See 'n Say lifestyle. My prayer is that I learn to *see* the blessings poured out around me every day—for instance, the daily kindnesses of Cami and Darice, my parents' caregivers—and to *say* how much I appreciate the lovingkindness they pour into our family. But too often I choose to see the negative and say what reflects negatively on God's reputation.

> ### *Roadside Rest*
> **SCRIPTURE FOR MEDITATION**
> When words are many, sin is not absent, but he who holds his tongue is wise (Proverbs 10:19).

Expressing appreciation should be my lifestyle. My daily prayer should be for eyes that are open to see where God is pouring out His blessings—in the big things and in the small—and for a spirit of gratitude.

Reinforce Biblical Truth

The battle in my heart recently was over the thermostat. The thought that raced through my mind as I readjusted the temperature for the third time (after my father had readjusted it) was, "But it's *my* thermostat in *my* house."

I could rationalize my thoughts—thoughts about boundaries and healthy relationships. And they would be good questions, worthy of pursuing. But the core question would remain. Was I thinking biblical truth? Isn't the thermostat in *my* home really my thermostat after all?

The answer to that question is both yes and no. Dan and I purchased this home, and it belongs to us. We are responsible for the heat bill and the taxes. We have rights of ownership, but we live here as a family with my parents. *Some like it hot; some like it cold* goes a long way in describing the thermostat needs of the assorted people who live in my house.

But there is a separate and even more important element in the equation. Everything Dan and I have belongs to God and must be viewed, first of all, as *His*.

It's important that as caregivers we're willing to submit our thinking, our presuppositions, our self-will, all that we have, to the truth of the Word of God. It can make for some complex realities in daily living. It can mean laying down our rights at times or lovingly confronting where no one else has been brave enough to confront before. But we must always make the Word of God the standard for our attitudes and conduct, not our personality, opinions, preferences, or our comfort level. We must learn to think biblically, speak biblically, walk biblically, and care biblically.

Intercept Negativity

As caregivers, it's easy to slip into negative patterns. Something inside of us wants to hear our frustrations reflected back to us and affirmed in the eyes of others. We sit in a Sunday school class and tell the details of how annoyingly a nurse treated us at the doctor's office. We call a sibling and share the story of how Mom or Dad acted in an inappropriate way, knowing that those details will inflame our sibling's already negative attitude toward our parent and justify our self-righteous frustrations.

But even though it's easy to slide into negativity, it's sinful. Although it's important to share useful information for a purpose, it's never important to share non-useful information for little or no purpose, and often we're tempted to do this because of our own frustrations. We need to learn to intercept negativity at the source—our attitude—and evaluate our motives and desires in sharing perceptions and information with others.

Evaluate Motives

Jeremiah 17:9 tells us, "The heart is deceitful above all things and beyond cure. Who can understand it?"

In spite of our desires to be selfless as we serve and care for those we love, we can trust our motives to become skewed, thanks to Eve's encounter with a serpent in the garden of Eden. None of us are above the lure of false and twisted motives.

Satan's devices daily slip into our motives and our attitudes, and he targets our hearts with his insidious intentions.

Greed.

Self-service.

Martyrdom.

Self-protection.

Pride.

At the center of human nature, we'll always struggle to serve ourselves first, to protect our rights, and, most of all, to question the goodness of God in the face of suffering. We'll face daily conflict in the caregiving battle. But we can be victorious. The old Marie in us can be transformed by applying simple principles drawn from Scripture.

If we focus first on magnifying God, on appreciating others, on reinforcing biblical truth, on intercepting negativity, and on evaluating our motives, we can learn to live above the level of frustration and spiritual subsistence. As we harness the power of praise and redemptive thinking, our hearts will change, our outlooks will change, and our relationships will change. We can walk in newness of life, clinging to the promise that God has promised to transform us into the image of His Son.

Marie Doesn't Live Here Any More: The Blessing of Change

One of the most encouraging truths my pastor shares repeatedly with our church family is that God's greatest gift to His children is change. Without change we are without hope. Without change, redemption is no more than a mirage.

As a caregiver, I am not a prisoner of my circumstances. I have not given up my freedom, but I have been given freedom—to be all that Christ created me to be in Him each day. I am not bound by duty, but I have been freed for service. God has called me to walk a path of challenge and of change, and I have found that with each step, I have been ambushed by grace and overwhelmed by blessing.

Prayer

Gracious heavenly Father, I come to you and ask you to convict me of my false motives and twisted thinking. Help me to see my greed, my self-service, my attitude of martyrdom, my self-protection, and my pride. May your Holy Spirit shine the light of truth into the darkest recesses of my heart and reveal the attitudes that I've hidden from myself for so long. Father, I desire change. I long for a renewed heart and a renewed spirit.

Precious Lord, may I learn to magnify you, to appreciate others, to reinforce biblical thinking, to intercept negativity, and to evaluate my motives. May I look deeply at each of these areas in my life as I seek to grow more into the image of your Son.

Meditation and Personal Application Questions

1. Can you relate to Rachel and Paul's circumstances? Do you ever feel stuck or like you're a prisoner of your circumstances? How do you deal with these feelings?
2. What aspects of your motives do you feel you struggle with most in your caregiving and why? How have you tried to deal with these issues on a spiritual level?
3. In what ways do you struggle with misuse of your tongue (complaining, disseminating negative impressions of others, reflecting negativity on people's character, expressing resentment, pride, and a bad attitude). What steps do you think God desires you to take to deal with these areas?
4. How does trusting in the character of God impact our motives?
5. What steps do you need to take to intercept negativity in your thinking?

Scripture for Further Meditation

1 Corinthians 4:3–5
James 4:3
1 Chronicles 28:9

Resources

Need a break? Consider the following resources from appendix 1: *www.alzstore.com* or *www.videorespite.com* for videos and other resources for those with Alzheimer's and dementias. Then for yourself, try *www.aarp.org/games* for online game resources.

I do not understand what I do.

For what I want to do I do not do, but what I hate I do.

And if I do what I do not want to do,

I agree that the law is good.

As it is, it is no longer I myself who do it,

but it is sin living in me.

I know that nothing good lives in me, that is,

in my sinful nature.

For I have the desire to do what is good,

but I cannot carry it out.

For what I do is not the good I want to do;

no, the evil I do not want to do—this I keep on doing.

ROMANS 7:15–19

Chapter Six

Pulling Out the Family Refrigerator

DEALING WITH GUILT AND GRIME

"I didn't expect to discover I could be a jealous sister when I was caring for my parents. My sister Shirley was the nurse—I was just a teacher, but Shirley lived five hours away. So when it came time to take care of Mom and Dad, the care fell to me.

"I quit my teaching when Mom and Dad's care got more intense. I felt like I had three full-time jobs then—our rental business, my parents, and my tutoring. For three years I took care of both Mom and Dad in their home. Then Mom died, and for three years I cared for Dad, ten months of that time in my home. He could be quite a handful, but I treasure the memories of those years.

"But what was hard was watching how my parents perked up when Shirley came home. It was like she was the special child, and I was just the daughter who took care of them every day. The jealousy was difficult. I know those years must have been even harder for my sister because she couldn't be here to help. I didn't want to be jealous, but it was a reality I had to face."

Barb

My mother was always a voracious housekeeper. She meticulously dusted light-bulbs, whacked rugs, and vacuumed the deepest recesses of her furniture as though trying to exorcise the upholstery of the evils of dust.

One of my mother's sacred housecleaning routines involved slipping an old T-shirt over the end of a yardstick and swirling it beneath the stove and refrigerator in order to rid our house of yet more evil dust. But because that alone wasn't enough, several times a year Mom and I would pull out the fridge and wash the floor until it was squeaky clean, then carefully vacuum the coils on the back of the refrigerator.

Vacuuming the refrigerator coils was something that separated the prudent from the wastrel in our home. My father believed that not dusting the coils would cause our electric bill to soar. Cleanliness was not only next to godliness in our family, it was worth cold hard cash. But I had come to believe that inattention to dusty refrigerator coils could lead to far more than the economic demise of my family. Our home might burst into flames in the middle of the night, and our entire family might burn to death in our beds. So when Dan and I got married, guilt should have driven me to rush out and purchase a yardstick. But as the weeks ticked by, the stark truth began to slowly settle upon me, like a shroud upon a corpse.

If you're looking for a way to get started helping your parent get organized, consult appendix 5 at the back of the book: "A Caregiver's Starter List of Helpful Tasks."

My coils were dirty. I was a slacker—a dirty slacker who was wasting God's money and who would probably burn in her bed beside her newlywed husband one night as payment for her sins.

Yet, even with this knowledge, I didn't buy the yardstick. I just lived with the guilt—until it caught up with me a year later.

Dan and I had finally gathered together enough money to move out of our apartment and into our first real home. I was elated. Until the horrible day a neighborhood friend, someone so neat she ironed her shoelaces, showed up to help me clean out our apartment and volunteered to pull out the refrigerator.

The desire to run flashed through my mind, but I had nowhere to go. The hidden goo and the grime of my life would be exposed, right there in front of a neat-freak deacon's wife. The mess I had worked so hard to shove out of my thinking would send this woman fleeing, I was certain. Once she saw me for the housekeeping failure I had pronounced myself to be, she would run screaming from my apartment (and for the nearest tetanus booster) and never return.

I was doomed.

And all because I had never learned to face my own spiritual dust bunnies.

How Dust Bunnies Are Born: Sources of Guilt

Stick a yardstick under a caregiver's family refrigerator, and it may get so stuck in the goo of family guilt that it may be hard to pull it back out. Sources of guilt for caregivers can multiply and skitter like dust bunnies on a breezy spring day. Guilt seems to be the hidden grime in the corner of every caregiver's life. And it's often among the list of things caregivers talk least about.

Dysfunctional or abusive family dynamics.
Unrealistic expectations.
Conflicting priorities.

Roadside Realities

"Experts say adults coping with an aged parent struggle with a range of emotions. Ambivalence is common—even a good relationship doesn't prevent mixed feelings. There's often some anger and resentment as unresolved family issues resurface. And there's plenty of guilt."

SHARON JAYSON, "Caregivers Cope with Stress,
Mixed Emotions," *USA TODAY*

Unmet needs.
Unclear boundaries.
Unresolved resentments.
Self-imposed criticism.
Other-imposed criticism.
Childhood fears.
Sibling rivalries.

These are the dust motes of the past and present that swirl about our lives and settle in with the grease and grime of everyday obligations and commitments. They're the realities of living in a world of sin and tension, conflict and chaos. As caregivers, we live in this tension, often feeling responsible for making the loved ones we care for happy, for alleviating their pain, for shaping the course of their final years, and for making their death as comfortable as possible, all while balancing the responsibilities of our families, our spiritual lives, our jobs, our social lives, and everything else life brings. Yet we often feel sideswiped by the inevitability of conflict. After all, we've been told that what God calls us to do, He equips us to accomplish and that we can expect His enablement in all things.

"Seek counseling to work through unresolved family of origin issues, such as physical, sexual, and emotional abuse or injury."

CHARLES PUCHTA,
Blessed Are the Caregivers, Aging America Resources, 2002–2004

But the truth of the Christian life is that we live in continual tension. We're to expect conflict. The Bible makes it clear that in this world we're to expect tribulation (James 1:2, 12). We're to earnestly contend for the faith (Jude 3), knowing that our sufficiency in all things is in God (Jude 24). When we look at the lives of the most heroic biblical characters—New Testament or Old—we see the reality of lives lived within the tension of conflict.

The life of the caregiver is not easy, and our responsibilities and roles will clash. It is in the tension that our motives and goals are refined as God shapes us.

Stepping Stones and Stumbling Blocks: True Guilt and False Guilt

Scripture uses a number of terms in regard to the word *guilt*. In many instances (Job 33:9–11; Matthew 5:22; Luke 23:4) these words encompass a sense of offense or iniquity, of culpability or responsibility in wrongdoing. In some cases, this type of guilt may apply to the caregiver. For instance, a broken or unrestored relationship between a parent and child can cause guilt. When this is true, God instructs us to confess our sins (1 John 1:9) and seek restoration with the other individuals in the relationship (Matthew 18:15–17).

This type of guilt is a manifestation of *true guilt*. True guilt involves responsibility for wrong actions that are worthy of blame and subsequent consequences.

Wherever we're responsible and feel true guilt because of our actions in a relationship, we're responsible for biblical repentance

---

Roadside Assistance

"If we do not choose to address the unfairness, irresponsibility, and the lack of love (which we sometimes call 'unfinished business'), we have a tendency to carry anger, bitterness, and hurt into other relationships. A great deal of damage can occur when we carry these unhealthy traits into relationships with our children, which in turn leaves them scarred and insecure."

TERRY D. HARGRAVE,
Loving Your Parents When They Can No Longer Love You

---

and restoration. God always intends for guilt to be a stepping stone to action. Like the pain of a sliver festering beneath our skin, guilt signals that something is wrong that needs to be made right.

Taking steps toward repentance and restoration means first confessing our sins (1 John 1:9) to God and to the individual we sinned against. Whether we receive the forgiveness of the individual we sinned against, we stand forgiven in God's sight and can live a life of freedom, as Colossians 2:7 states, "rooted and built up in him, strengthened in the faith as [we] were taught, and overflowing with thankfulness." Jesus Christ has made the payment for our sin, and we are no longer under condemnation (Romans 8:1). It then becomes our life goal to live out the double-love command in regard to that individual.

The Dust Bunnies Speak: Listening to Our Guilt

It's important to listen to our guilt and recognize whether we're dealing with true guilt stemming from an offense that we're responsible for or *false guilt* stemming from self-condemnation or the weight of trying to live up to the expectations of others. Do we feel guilt because of an action we've committed? Or do we feel guilt because of an expectation that others have placed on us? Is our guilt stemming from the way we perceive ourselves to be? Are others blaming us? Are we blaming ourselves? Is the issue a matter of right or wrong, or is it only a matter of expectations?

Roadside Rest

SCRIPTURE FOR MEDITATION

If we confess our sins, he is faithful and just and will forgive us our sins and purify us from all unrighteousness (1 John 1:9).

False guilt may be the greatest struggle caregivers share. Those we care for, our immediate family, and sometimes extended family members place expectations upon us. The parents we're caring for may make poor decisions that we're forced to override but that run contrary to their desires. Or perhaps we're not able to schedule time off work to accompany our loved ones to all of their doctor's appointments. Maybe we're missing our children's sporting events or time with our spouse.

False guilt isn't based on our moral actions of good or bad, right or wrong, but upon our desires to live up to someone else's expectations of us or of our expectations of ourselves. When we're plagued by false guilt, we're attempting to

> *Roadside Assistance*
>
> "The care recipient has the right and responsibility to make all decisions as long as they have the mental capacity to do so."
>
> CHARLES PUCHTA, *Blessed Are the Caregivers*, AGING AMERICA RESOURCES, 2004–2005

perform to a standard of expectations in order to measure up. But like the dust bunnies beneath the bed, when we try to sweep the responsibilities of our lives into a neat pile, the clumps and clusters sometimes skitter away and hide in the nooks and crannies, only to peek out later, when we least expect them.

It's important to ask evaluative questions when we feel the grip of guilt pressing in. As we look at our circumstances and our attitudes, we should attempt to discern between true guilt and false guilt.

- Is the source of my guilt from a sinful action or attitude I'm responsible for?
- Have I violated a principle or command of Scripture in my conduct or attitude?
- Is the source of my guilt from an unrealistic expectation or perfectionism?
- Is the source of my guilt the condemning attitude of others?
- Is the source of my guilt self-condemnation?
- Is the source of my guilt the accusing voice of Satan?
- Am I relying upon my works or service for others to gain the approval of others?

- Am I capable of fulfilling all the demands or responsibilities placed upon me by others?
- Am I willing to rest in the knowledge that I'm asked to earnestly *contend* (Jude 3), yet *rest*, knowing that my *sufficiency* in all things is in God (Jude 24)?
- Am I capable of seeing myself as beloved in the Father, embraced and adored, in spite of my performance?

Swirling the Yardstick: Finding Answers

My pantry closet boasts a number of newfangled floor cleaning devices, each with its own assigned nail or clip, thanks to the engineering acumen of my father, the patience of my husband, and the organizational skills of my daughter. Two Swiffer Sweepers hang side-by-side, one for dry floors and one for wet. I am also the proud owner of an angled broom, with its own cleverly attached dustpan, and a cute yellow whisk broom. But none of these floor-cleaning devices will do the job of cleaning under my refrigerator. To do that, I must slip an old T-shirt onto a yardstick and swirl it about beneath the fridge. In forty years, no one has invented anything better. Sometimes only the old-fashioned simple things work best.

When it comes to caregiver guilt, we all must face a few realities. The first is that Satan is the great accuser, and if he can burden us with guilt for serving and loving, he will find a way to do it. John 16:33 promises us that we will struggle in this world, and we will face difficulty: "I have told you these things, so that in me you may have peace. In this world you will have trouble. But take heart! I have overcome the world." As believers, we find our hope in the cross. Our task is to take up our cross daily and to serve (Luke 9:23), knowing our sufficiency is in God, and we lack no good thing.

Dealing with the realities of guilt often means dealing with the realities of daily life. It means, first and foremost, searching our hearts for sources of true guilt, confessing them, and seeking reconciliation and restoration with those around us. It means, second, that we must evaluate the voices of our guilt and unmask the sources of false guilt. As we do, we need to obliterate Satan's lies, and then replace those lies with the truth of the Word of God as we draw closer to Him and as He helps us establish healthier, more God-honoring priorities.

Is our spiritual life our first priority? Are we in the Word? Are we accountable and in a body of believers where we are regularly being taught?

Have we consciously and thoughtfully established priorities, sorting through the have-to's and want-to's of our caregiving life and our personal life? Have we discussed these priorities with immediate family members and the loved one we're caring for? With extended family members?

Are we attending to our own health concerns? Are we getting appropriate rest? Respite? Medical attention? Are we eating a healthy diet? Getting enough exercise? Are we experiencing fatigue or depression?

Are we making room for our social needs? Do we see friends and maintain relationships? Do we involve ourselves with hobbies? Are we involved with support groups? Have we created "spaces" in our life for ourselves?

Are the financial boundaries in our caregiving situation clearly delineated and equitable to everyone concerned, or do they cause frustration? Have we searched for and asked for financial assistance from sources where it may be available?

Have we established healthy relational boundaries in our caregiving situation? Do we ask for and expect respect, and do we model respect in our relationships with others? Have we sought counseling for unresolved, critical, or abusive situations? Have we been guilty of crossing unhealthy lines in our relationships, and do we need to repent of those things and seek restoration?

Guilt is God's spiritual cattle prod. It is intended to move us forward. Guilt is often one way the Holy Spirit tells us to quit sitting around and to get up and find a T-shirt and a yardstick.

God doesn't intend for us to do everything. He is not a perfectionist or a taskmaster. He is a proud Father who dotes on His children. He delights in us, like a mother who becomes lost in the beauty of the gaze of her newborn child.

He does not heap guilt upon us but came to take our guilt and our shame so that we could walk in freedom.

Even in our imperfection.

Prayer

Father God, I confess that I often struggle with the weight of guilt for what I do and what I do not do. Help me to discern between the true guilt and false guilt in my life and to learn even from that. May I have a heart that is sensitive to sin. Help me to see where I have offended and where I need to repent and seek restoration with those around me. And help me to silence the voice of false guilt with the truth of your Word and who I am in you.

Father, help me to establish priorities that honor you. Help me to find balance in the tension and to lay my false guilt at your feet, knowing that it is not from you but that it is an instrument of Satan in my life to defeat me. Thank you for your empowerment to love and serve and to walk in freedom.

Meditation and Personal Application Questions

1. Can you relate to Barb's feelings of jealousy? In what ways? How would you have dealt with her situation?

2. What areas of false guilt have troubled you? Consider the following steps when you're dealing with false guilt:
   a. Identify the source and ask *why* you believe you're susceptible to this accusing message.
   b. Claim the finished atonement of Jesus Christ and the truth that your good works are only as filthy rags in God's eyes.
   c. Draw close to Jesus through prayer and meditation.
   d. Pray for cleansing and forgiveness (Romans 3:23; 10:13).
   e. Acknowledge that Satan is an accuser.
   f. Claim the fact that your sins are remembered no more (Jeremiah 31:34b).
3. What areas of imbalance in your life cause you the greatest source of guilt? What steps can you take to establish better balance in these areas?

Scripture for Further Meditation

Romans 8:1
1 Peter 2:24
Psalm 103:8–14

Resources

If you're overwhelmed by the level of care your loved one needs and you're in need of a free referral service, consider contacting your local Area Agency on Aging or any of the resources in appendix 1 at the back of the book.

Blessed are they who keep his statutes and
seek him with all their heart...
How can a young man keep his way pure?
By living according to your word...
I will walk about in freedom,
for I have sought out your precepts.

PSALM 119:2, 9, 45

Chapter Seven

Dancing on Fences

BUILDING BOUNDARIES

"I don't think anyone had ever stood up to my father-in-law before he came to live with us. He was quite a handful. But Gordon and I were committed to honoring his dad, and we needed to make it work for the whole family.

"I was the first person who ever faced my father-in-law with the reality of boundaries. It wasn't easy because some of his behavior was unacceptable, but there had to be a foundation of mutual honor and respect in order for him to live in our home. I can't say there wasn't some conflict, but he learned he had to make changes, and that was as good for him as it was for us."

Linda

Nothing gets your adrenaline flowing like herding a gaggle of high school students through a series of foreign countries whose traffic laws seem to have been written by a committee of second graders.

It is only by the grace of God that Tara, a student on one of the many travel-study trips I've conducted to Europe, isn't expanding her educational horizons on the streets of heaven, hunting down Aaron or Moses for a chat at this very moment. On one lovely Roman summer afternoon, Tara became distracted and forgot about the critical need for an awareness of boundaries—both hers and others'. As we strolled the cobbled streets near the Vatican, she stepped off a curb and into the pathway of a purple Vespa motorbike that was weaving in and out of tour buses, Tic-Tac-sized Euromobiles, and at least three thousand other scooters.

Amazingly, the Vespa bounced off Tara's hundred-and-ten pound frame like a super-powered Nerf ball, and the result, as the bike, driver, and Tara went flying in three different directions, reminded watchers of a scene from a Saturday morning cartoon with Italian subtitles.

While our other tour members (including me) screamed and flailed their arms, Tara sedately gathered herself, dusted off her skirt, and gave a gracious (if not slightly garbled) apology to the driver before re-absorbing herself into the frenzy of our panicked group.

For the remainder of the trip, Tara was newly aware of her surroundings—curbs, traffic lights, guardrails, stairs, even doorways. She was now personally aware of the advantages of looking both left *and* right when crossing the streets of London, of giving careful regard to zebra stripes painted near sidewalks, of avoiding roundabouts at all costs, and of always allowing someone else to be the first to step off the curb.

Tara had learned that boundaries are good, if you just learn to pay attention to them. They can keep you from getting flattened, and they can keep other people from getting bounced down the road along with you. The best boundaries are those that everyone knows and respects. Otherwise, boundaries can be pretty worthless, and people can end up contestants in an unexpected game of Wrinklefender with a Vespa, where everyone comes out the loser.

Family Wrinklefender: Battered Boundaries

Many of us stepped into caregiving roles with the best of intentions, glancing to the right and the left before stepping off the curb, thinking we've surveyed the situation and can cross to the other side without incident. But suddenly, out of nowhere, the clash of boundary expectations mowed us down. Some of us, like Tara, may have been able to dust ourselves off from the blow. Others may have dragged ourselves off, wounded. And still others may have packed their bags and called it quits.

We all come to caregiving dragging the baggage of our past behind us. We were all born into families with their own unique cultures, some perhaps more "functional" than others. But even the most amicable families struggle with boundaries—with what constitutes acceptable and unacceptable behavior, of who calls the shots for whom, of how physical, spiritual, and emotional health are defined and lived out.

For some of us, the word *boundary* may be a four-letter word. Laying down boundaries means saying no, drawing lines, facing today's realities, facing our past. It may mean facing fears and insecurities—our own as well as the fears and insecurities of those we love. For many of us, the word *boundary* means confrontation and change, and that may be the most frightening aspect of all.

But change can also be the most exciting aspect of understanding boundaries because change brings the expectation of hope. And without change, we have no hope.

Pulling Down the Stop Signs: The Hope of Our Image-Bearing

The amazing truth of creation and the incarnation is that God chose to place the stamp of His image within the hearts of all people. We all bear the indelible mark of God himself, and as His image bearers, we're all worthy of respect and honor, and we bear divine dignity. Jesus paid the price of redemption for all mankind. "Then God said, 'Let us make man in our image, in our likeness...' God created man in his own image, in the image of God he created him; male and female he created them" (Genesis 1:26–27). Because of our image-bearing, we all share in God's common grace that makes it possible for us to meet one another on the level ground of mutual respect. Our image-bearing makes it possible for us to work at establishing healthy and God-honoring boundaries in our relationships, boundaries that serve as an impetus to growth and as a protection for us and for those around us.

We can never learn to live responsibly in community until we learn to live with an understanding of personal consequences and our right and responsibility to steward the time, talents, and emotional, material, physical, and spiritual gifts God has given us. And this can only take place within the context of boundary setting.

Family Grime That Clings: The Need for Boundaries

"My mother is verbally abusive to everyone. She bosses everyone in the nursing home and demands that people jump to meet her every whim. She's constantly criticizing everyone. I'm embarrassed every time I go to visit her and interact with the staff because she treats them so rudely."

On a recent television call-in show, a guest phoned in and related her frustration. "My father has never shown respect to any of our family members, and I'm the only daughter. Dad's recently had a stroke, and now my brothers expect that he's automatically going to move in with me because they're all men. I feel like I don't have a right to say no. I don't even know how to approach the subject in a conversation with them."

> *Roadside Rest*
>
> **SCRIPTURE FOR MEDITATION**
>
> I have given them the glory that you gave me, that they may be one as we are one: I in them and you in me. May they be brought to complete unity to let the world know that you sent me and have loved them even as you have loved me (John 17:22–23).

When it comes to the issue of boundaries in families, to drawing lines and saying yes and no to the expectations of others, all caregiving families face challenges. The reason is simple: at one level or another, many of us are still children, cowering behind a living room chair listening as the front door slams and a parent leaves for the last time. Others of us may be standing in the kitchen with a report card in our hand, knowing we'll never measure up, wondering what we can do to please our parent just this once. Perhaps others are trying to negotiate the arguments between Mom and Dad or are trying to escape the deafening silence that marked our home.

Many of our patterns of interrelating in regard to boundaries can be traced to behaviors we learned in childhood that are rooted in our family relationships. Dr. Henry Cloud and Dr. John Townsend explore these relationships in their book *Boundaries: When to Say YES, When to Say NO to Take Control of Your Life* (Zondervan 1992). According to Drs. Townsend and Cloud,

> These patterns run deep. Your family members are the ones you learned to organize your life around, so they are able to send you back to old patterns by their very presence. You begin to act automatically out of *memory* instead of growth.

Roadside Assistance

"In a caregiving setting, it's important to negotiate clearly what each of you can and cannot do. For the caregiver, set boundaries around your time and availability. Give your loved one time to transition to changes. For the family member who has moved in, accept boundaries. Negotiate if they don't seem reasonable. Make every effort to be flexible when your caregiver introduces new activities or change."

MARIE HARTWELL-WALKER, *Caregiving Is a Two-Way Relationship*, HELPHORIZONS.COM, JULY 11, 2007

To change, you must identify these "sins of the family" and turn from them. You must confess them as sins, repent of them, and change the way you handle them. The first step in establishing boundaries is becoming aware of old family patterns that you are still continuing in the present.[1]

Becoming aware of old family patterns is difficult work but critical work—to caregiving but, more importantly, to spiritual and emotional maturity.

Biblical Roots: The Importance of Boundaries

It's important to understand the biblical basis of boundaries and the role they play in relationships. According to Townsend and Cloud, "Biblical boundaries help you achieve the relationships and purposes God intends for you as his child."[2] Boundaries delineate what will flow both in and out of our lives. They are the parameters that give shape and purpose to our interactions with others and our choices. Without boundaries in our physical lives, our emotional and relational lives, and our spiritual lives, we would live at the whim and control of others and at the whim of our sinful natures. Boundaries tell others how far they can go and tell us how far we are willing to go.

When my brother Paul and I were young, my dad gave Paul permission to build a fort on our extra back lot and call it his own. But like the sinful little sister I was, I loved to sneak into Paul's fort (daddy longlegs and all) and sit in the darkness, just to know I was trespassing. Something inside me called out to me to violate Paul's space. On the days when I crawled out of his carefully constructed

---

1. Dr. Henry Cloud and Dr. John Townsend, *Boundaries: When to Say YES, When to Say NO to Take Control of Your Life* (Grand Rapids, Michigan: Zondervan, 1992), 131.

2. *Boundaries: When to Say YES, When to Say NO to Take Control of Your Life*, 26.

Roadside Assistance

Several overarching principles apply to boundaries in a care-giving setting. First of all, the life ability of care receivers must be considered. What are they capable of? What can they be held responsible for? The goal is to make people responsible for what they are capable of and to move them out of their comfort zone but to keep them within their ability zone. Second, the shared expectations of the household should apply to everyone as much as possible and should be discussed and possibly even written out. Thirdly, allow maximum freedom for the individual being cared for, depending upon their level of responsibility.

DR. JOHN TOWNSEND, INTERVIEW

hole in the ground, more than physical dirt clung to me as I snuck back to the house. Sin stuck to my soul.

God established clear boundaries in His relationship with mankind. He established boundaries for the created order and for mankind's rule over creation. He established clear expectations for our conduct and consequences for self-centered and sinful behavior. He established boundaries in governmental structures and the marriage relationship. He established boundaries for the manner in which redemption would come into the world, and He created people in His image, who, like himself, would function best within society and within their relationships with the protection and blessing of boundaries.

The Building Blocks: Basic Steps to Boundary Building

A number of key principles apply to boundary building and can be derived from an application of the double-love command, which is rooted in our commitment to pursue the best good for those we love from pure motives.

- **Autonomy**. After God created Adam and Eve, He gave mankind the freedom to pursue moral choices, along with the subsequent responsibility of facing the consequences for their choices. "And the Lord God commanded the man, 'You are free to eat from any tree in the garden; but you must not eat from the tree of the knowledge of good and evil, for when you eat of it you will surely die" (Genesis 2:16–17).

As caregivers, we must sometimes make the difficult assessment of whether our loved ones have reached or are reaching the end of their capacity of making informed and healthy decisions for themselves. But in cases where parents are still mentally alert, we must respect their right to make life decisions for themselves. However, if their life decisions are producing consequences that negatively impact the lives of others, we must pursue the most effective means to negotiate.

Right now my father, who has a pacemaker, is in the front yard playing tug-of-war with a dead pine tree and a block-and-tackle. Dad knows he has a bad heart. I know he has a bad heart. We've talked about the dangers of his overexerting. But my father delights in feeling useful, and Dan and I hover over him but allow him to make decisions about home projects. We have no desire that my father die a premature death, but we do desire that he feel like an *elder*, and not *elderly*. And so we allow him autonomy in these choices. However, if he were choosing to abuse our house rules or to be emotionally or physically abusive, that would be an entirely different matter. Those boundaries would cross into the welfare and safety of our family, and that would require, at the least, negotiation.

- **Negotiation.** Scripture gives numerous examples of negotiation to arbitrate difficult circumstances. God himself negotiated with Abraham in Genesis 18 for the plight of Sodom.

Proverbs 15:22 exhorts the believer regarding the wisdom of counsel: "Plans fail for lack of counsel, but with many advisers they succeed."

In his book *The Peacemaker: A Biblical Guide to Resolving Personal Conflict*, author Ken Sande provides five key principles to biblical negotiation, called the Pause Principle:

P Prepare, pray, get the facts, seek godly counsel, and look for options.

A Affirm relationships. Show genuine concern and respect for others.

U Understand interests. Identify with others' concerns, desires, needs, limitations, and fears.

S Search for creative solutions. Brainstorm.

E Evaluate options objectively and reasonably (evaluate, don't argue).[3]

These simple principles can help caregivers work through steps of negotiation as they bathe their efforts in prayer.

My friend folded her arms and leaned across the restaurant table as she talked to me about her mother, who had recently moved in with her.

"She simply won't lift a finger to do anything for herself. She has far more physical capability than most of the older folks in our church, but we can't get her to contribute in any way to our household since she's moved in. She stays in her room all day and expects us to wait on her."

One important element of negotiation might have been for my friend to discuss family expectations before her mom moved in and to have written down what her contribution to the family would be after a time of transition. One option might have been to give

---

3. Ken Sande, *The Peacemaker: A Biblical Guide to Resolving Personal Conflict* (Grand Rapids: Baker Books, 1997), Peacemaker Ministries, www.peacemaker.net. Used by permission.

her a choice of several simple household tasks that she could select from and have her choose three that would be her responsibility, explaining that everyone in the family is expected to make a contribution within their ability level. But whatever boundaries would have been set in place would have required consequences on my friend's part and perhaps an eventual discussion with her mother about the need for her to find an alternate living arrangement if she couldn't live within the reasonable expectations of their home.

Roadside Assistance

See "Suggestions for Decision-Making and Compromise," appendix 10, for additional resources on negotiation.

But it is *not* unloving or unbiblical to hold loved ones accountable for their actions and to expect them to respect the rules of the home as other family members are expected to.

- **Respect.** Leviticus 19:32 states, "Rise in the presence of the aged, show respect for the elderly and revere your God. I am the Lord." This same chapter says, "Each of you must respect his mother and father, and you must observe my Sabbaths. I am the Lord your God (v. 3)." In each of these passages, respect for family members and reverence for God are placed in the same context. Mutual respect must be an element of our boundary setting, as we seek the best interests of those we love and serve.

First Peter 3:8–9 provides further commentary on our mutual submission: "Finally, all of you, live in harmony with one another; be sympathetic, love as brothers, be compassionate and humble. Do not repay evil with evil or insult with insult, but with blessing, because to this you were called so that you may inherit a blessing."

The key elements of this passage encapsulate a heart of respect: striving for harmony, cultivating a sympathetic heart, loving as brothers, showing compassion and humility, and pouring out the blessing of grace.

It is important to understand that respect is not conciliation. It is commitment to the best interests of your loved one as carried out in the double-love command.

- **Listening**. Boundary setting involves a listening heart—a heart that can listen to both what is spoken and what is unspoken. James 1:19 explains, "My dear brothers, take note of this: Everyone should be quick to listen, slow to speak and slow to become angry."

Several key principles apply to the art of listening well. First, acknowledge the feelings and emotions of the person you are speaking to. Rephrase or restate that person's feelings in order to create connection and understanding. Show empathy, not just sympathy. Empathy means that you're meeting people on their emotional level and not condescending to their feelings with a simple, "I'm sorry." Avoid judgments and ask open-ended questions.

In his book *The Seven Habits of Highly Effective People*, author Stephen Covey shares a simple but profound principle of listening: Seek first to understand, then to be understood. We can do this by checking our motives and the actual process we bring to listening. Are we ignoring the other people's responses as they speak, mentally and emotionally condescending to their thoughts and feelings? Are we simply preparing our next answer or rebuttal? Are we giving the illusion of actually listening, or are we truly engaged in the process? Are we attentive and engaged? Do our body language, tone, facial expressions, and word choices communicate authentic concern?

Experts tell us that only a fraction of our communication rests upon the words we speak. The vast majority of meaning we portray is carried by our tone, our facial expression, and the nuances of our body language.

What are you *really* saying when you think you're listening?

- **Honesty.** Psalm 15:1–5 summarizes the walk of the man of integrity—the man of honesty:

"Lord, who may dwell in your sanctuary? Who may live on your holy hill? He whose walk is blameless and who does what is righteous, who speaks the truth from his heart and has no slander on his tongue, who does his neighbor no wrong and casts no slur on his fellowman, who despises a vile man but honors those who fear the Lord, who keeps his oath even when it hurts,who lends his money without usury and does not accept a bribe against the innocent. He who does these things will never be shaken."

The godly man in this passage is clearly a man who has drawn clear boundaries that delineate who he is and who he is not. He is a man of honesty and righteousness who speaks the truth yet guards his tongue. He has set boundaries of respect in word, deed, and attitude toward his fellowmen. He delineates in his attitude between good and evil men. He does what is right and keeps his word without regard for personal cost. He is a steward of his money and possessions and seeks appropriate return on his investment, yet he doesn't take advantage of others. He is not a pushover. He walks in confidence, placing high expectations on himself and on those around him. He is a man who knows the value of boundaries. And God places His stamp of approval upon him: "He who does these things will never be shaken."

The man of Psalm 15 is a role model for boundary setting. He walks in a world of clearly delineated expectations and boundaries based upon objective truth. And he expects righteous behavior from those around him. As a man of integrity, he is considered a man worthy of being a houseguest in the sanctuary of God himself.

- **Expectations and consequences.** Galatians 6:7–8 is clear about God's expectations in regard to sowing and reaping: "Do not be deceived: God cannot be mocked. A man reaps what he sows. The one who sows to please his sinful nature, from that nature will reap destruction; the one who sows to please the Spirit, from the Spirit will reap eternal life." The natural order of life after the fall of man was that sin would produce consequences. Yet when we love someone, we often feel that the loving thing to do is to defer the consequences of wrong actions for those we care for rather than to let the painful consequences play out in their lives.

In boundary setting it's important to remember that we establish clear expectations from the beginning. All members of a family unit should be responsible for adhering to the same core values and practices within the family. And where those boundaries are crossed, consequences should be clearly spelled out. But those consequences must be carried out in our behaviors in ways that we can control, not in the behaviors of our loved ones, which we are not responsible for controlling.

A friend told me about her father's pattern of disrespectful speech throughout his life. He was often critical and harsh, and when he moved into Jean's home, she knew she would need to lay down clear boundaries regarding his disrespectful speech. She knew it might be difficult to change his behavior through establishing boundaries, but she knew she had to tell him her expectations and what the consequences would be if they were not met.

Jean's father didn't like the style of worship in their contemporary church, and soon after he moved in with Jean and her husband, he began to cite his criticisms. Jean and her husband sat down with her father one afternoon and respectfully explained that it was unloving and unbiblical to be critical of their church. They felt it was important to be God-honoring in their speech, and they would expect this standard of their father in their home as well since he was a believer. If it distressed him to attend their church with them, he was free to remain at home and find an acceptable program on television.

Then Jean waited for the purple Vespa to mow her down and leave her bloody body in a heap in the street. No one had ever confronted her father before or held him accountable. In over eighty years, no one had ever set a boundary for him and made him stay on his side of the line.

And much to Jean's surprise, her father complied. And he not only complied, over the next few months, he began to comment on how much he liked the sound of the steel guitar. On occasion he claimed to get "swept up" in the music.

His critical comments began to fade away. And he began to take on more of the image of the father Jean had always envisioned him to be.

We can dance on the fences, knowing they are not what divide us, but, ultimately, part of what binds us.

Prayer

Dear gracious heavenly Father, thank you for the boundaries that protect me in my life. Thank you for being a God who has spelled out who you are and who you are not, what you accept and what you do not accept. Thank you for loving us just as we are but so much that you do not leave us as we are.

Teach me to listen selflessly, to negotiate wisely, to lay down boundaries that serve purposes of building up and growing those I love, of loving and protecting them but not enabling them and sheltering them from the consequences of their actions.

Father, help me to see that boundaries are an impetus to change and growth and to desire that in my own life first of all.

Meditation and Personal Application Questions

1. What family patterns of behavior have you organized your life around that make it difficult for you to set healthy boundaries in your caregiving?
2. How can the PAUSE Principle help you take steps to establish better boundaries in the future?
3. What steps can you take to improve your listening skills? Your negotiation skills? What insight do these Scriptures shed on our listening and keys to gaining wisdom:
    a. Proverbs 12:15
    b. Proverbs 13:10
4. Do you show respect toward others and expect it in return? How can you work to create an atmosphere of mutual respect in your home, based upon the biblical principle of image-bearing?
5. What expectations and consequences have you laid down in your caregiving situation, and how have you followed through with those consequences? Do you feel these approaches have been effective? Why or why not?

Scripture for Further Meditation

John 15:12
Psalm 15:1–5
James 4:1–2

Recommended Resources

Boundaries: When to Say YES, When to Say NO to Take Control of Your Life by Drs. Henry Cloud and John Townsend (Zondervan, 1992).

The Peacemaker: A Biblical Guide to Resolving Personal Conflict by Ken Sande (Grand Rapids: Baker Books, 1997).

The Word became flesh and made his dwelling among us.
We have seen his glory, the glory of the One and Only,
who came from the Father,
full of grace and truth...
From the fullness of his grace we have all received
one blessing after another.
For the law was given through Moses;
grace and truth came through Jesus Christ.

JOHN 1:14, 16–17

Chapter Eight

Swapping Thimbles for a Mack Truck

LEARNING TO BE GRACE DUMPERS

"My husband walked out on me just months after we learned that our daughter had a terminal disease. She isn't expected to live another year. She requires twenty-four-hour care, and every day I lose a little bit more of her.

"It took too much out of him to watch her dying, so he left. He'll never know what he missed. Every day with her is a blessing. I'll never regret what I'm doing. Right now my whole life is caring for her. It's no accident we named her Grace. I've only got a small sliver of time before God takes her home, so every day I have with her is special. Remembering that is what keeps me focused."

Noreen

⌐

The balking began as I slid Mom out of the van in front of the automatic doors. I had learned to hate rubber floor mats. And patterned carpets. And zebra-striped sidewalks. And geometric floor tiles. And large open spaces that narrowed to small doorways. They all seemed to trigger something in Mom's brain that told her legs to freeze. But I managed to gently cajole her through the door of the grocery store as people stepped politely around us.

She balked again as we reached the greeter, overwhelmed by the bright lights, scurrying crowds, and jumbled voices. It was a confusing environment for someone with Alzheimer's, but it was one of the few places I could take Mom and Dad for a walk in the winter months. Some days we compromised and put Mom in a wheelchair for part of our visit. On her "bad" days we strolled the aisles with her in the chair while Dad circled the store like a speed walker in training.

Mom and I meandered through the produce department and selected a few fresh vegetables and some bulk nuts and raisins. I pulled the cart from the front, steering it as she pushed it from behind, but within minutes she began to complain that she was cold. She was always cold, in spite of the jacket I had zipped into place as soon as we had entered. Dad knew he would be able to find us on our bench near the Starbucks after he had made his purchases, so we made our way to the closest check-out. Only one customer stood between us and the bench near Starbucks, and I shot a thank-you heavenward.

The woman in front of us had only halfway unloaded her order from her cart, and groceries were piled high on the conveyor belt waiting to be scanned. Mom stood beside me as I slowly handed items to her to place on the belt, hoping that if she helped, she wouldn't grow restless.

A woman with a toddler in her cart slid into line behind us as Mom and I worked methodically to unload our groceries. As the young mother flashed her child a loving look, my gaze froze in horror.

My eyes searched for a way of escape, but there was none. I couldn't move forward. The woman in front of me was blocking our path. And I couldn't back out without passing directly by the woman and child who had just pulled into line behind us.

I glanced back into my cart. Only three items remained in the bottom. How long could I distract my mother with three items?

In the end, it didn't matter. Mom turned slowly and faced the woman and baby behind us—a lovely young African American mother and her little girl.

My heart sank as I saw Mom's face brighten.

"A baby. Isn't she beautiful?"

I felt my throat constrict as I placed my hand on my mother's arm and tried to turn her. "Yes, she *is* beautiful. Help me unload the cart, Mom."

Mom continued to smile at the baby, then at the mother. "You have a beautiful baby. A beautiful little..." I winced as the racial slur fell from her lips. Mom's smile was as loving as the word was ugly.

It felt like minutes before I had the courage to look up.

The mother was young—twenty-five at the oldest. Her gaze held steady, and she never blinked. She leaned toward me as she spoke, slowly and deliberately.

"We took care of my Grandmama for almost ten years before she passed. She was sick, too. I know what it's like when someone you love is sick." She smiled, and in that moment my fear was erased, and my heart was ambushed by grace.

Where I feared reprisal, I received unmerited favor.

Where I feared anger, I received kindness.

Where I felt shame, I received fellowship in suffering.

Grace gave this beautiful mother the vision not to define my mother by her words or her actions. Instead, grace gave her the ability to envision her as God saw her.

Grace sees past our faults. It sees beyond the surface of who we are to who God intends us to be. Grace says, "I know who I am, and because of that, I'm empowered to see who God intended you to be. I am empowered to freely give and to forgive."

Grace has a beauty all its own—a beauty that flows freely upon others.

A Picture of Beauty: Portrait of a Grace Dumper

I stood breathless that day and stared into the eyes of grace and the face of a young mother's quiet assurance. In that moment I was newly aware of the pet grievances I had clutched to my heart, like the tattered blue blanket we had wrested from my son at the age of three.

Resentments I stroked in the darkness of night for comfort.

Rebuttals I caressed like a favorite toy.

Self-justifications that echoed with the hollow tones of a child's nursery rhyme.

Her passion told me that her confidence did not rest in the words of others, but in her confidence of the truth, in her knowledge of who she was. She knew grace, and, therefore, she could share it. She could give what she had at one point received. She was an example of the stark contrast between those who lavish grace on those around them and those who live with the misconception that they can hoard what was never intended to be kept. Our lives were intended to be conduits of grace. The moment we believe we can hoard the grace we've received, it dissipates from our life and is gone.

For me, the word *grace* will always be represented by the face of a young African American mother who chose to look beyond unloveliness and see the beauty that God and I see.

Hoarding Versus Dumping: Trading Our Thimbles for Mack Trucks

Note the contrast between the grace hoarders and the grace dumpers.

Grace Hoarders	Grace Dumpers
Judge others	Look beyond the faults of others
Condemn others	Forgive others
Are threatened by the injustice of others	Stand firm in the knowledge of their identity
See failings when they look at others	See God's identity & vision for others' lives
Speak to defend themselves and pronounce judgment on others	Speak to give life and hope to others

The grace dumper looks to Calvary to find history's most lavish gift of grace poured out on all mankind. It was there that Jesus looked beyond our faults and forgave the sins of the entire world, empowered by His identity as the true and living Son of God. As the Alpha and Omega, the beginning and the end, He secured our eternal salvation. He alone sees our true identity and the vision for which we were created and speaks life and hope to us through the gift of His Holy Spirit and His Holy Word, the Bible. It is through the life-giving grace of God that we can live lives of purpose and have a hope for eternity. And it is this same grace that we can pass on as a free gift in the lives of others: the gift of forgiveness, vision, hope, and life affirmation. It's this power that gives us the ability to live lives of grace in a graceless world, in spite of our circumstances.

The Vision of Grace:
Swapping Forgiveness for Reprisal

One of the most difficult things for adult children to deal with is the failings of their parents. Most of us can point to hurts and offenses in our pasts—some of the "Ward and June Cleaver" variety, some that would qualify for an episode of *Criminal Minds*. And as amazing as it might sound, one category of offense is not necessarily less painful to deal with than the other.

> "The call of grace is to live a gracious life. For that is how grace works."
> MAX LUCADO,
> *In the Grip of Grace,* 117

A friend of mind learned not long ago that her elderly father, a church-going man, had molested several of his grandchildren. The ensuing family meetings did not go well, and the family struggled for years through layers of issues that exposed raw roots of emotion.

Another close friend has a father who remarried in his seventies, just a few months after his first wife passed away after a prolonged bout with cancer. Although my friend loves her new stepmother, she hasn't been able to adjust to the shock of her father's remarriage so soon after her mother's death, especially since the woman her father married was someone he had known and worked with for thirty years. The timing of the remarriage seemed like a betrayal of her mother. And when did her father take an interest in his second wife, anyway?

What would it mean to be a grace dumper in each of these situations and follow Jesus' example? And should we even want to? Can't slathering indiscriminate grace around a fallen world mean enabling the sinful behaviors of those around us?

The Heavenly Trifecta: Three *Whys* of Grace

There's nothing quite as unappealing as a spiritually and emotionally immature adult. You can be certain that if you know a spiritually immature adult, you know someone who doesn't understand grace.

Demanding, manipulative, incapable of playing well with others, always needing to be the center of attention.

Perhaps you know a few of these folks. Perhaps your parent is one and is living in your home or in a nursing home across the street. Or perhaps *you're* one. If you have your doubts, consider taking a survey about yourself and asking a few friends because it would be worth your while to find out and literally get a new life—a life of freedom and forgiveness—while God extends you the opportunity.

One of the most amazing aspects of our role as conduits of God's grace is that we get something in return: freedom and maturity. This spiritual maturity is the first *why* of grace. James 1:4 tells us, "Perseverance must finish its work *so that you may be mature and complete, not lacking anything*" [emphasis added]. Romans 6:22 tells us that as mature believers, we become slaves to God, and that "the benefit you reap leads to holiness." Holiness, then, works itself out in the image of Christ lived out in our lives. As we walk in Him, we become spiritually mature and begin to unclench our fists, release the reins of control, step out of the center, and see others, perhaps for the first time, as God sees them.

The second *why* of grace is that it is our only hope for reconciliation. Apart from grace, we remain spiritually separated from God, emotionally severed from others, and physically compromised in our health. Grace is a balm of healing on wounds and scars—even if reconciliation never takes place. The healing power of grace is twofold: it holds life-changing power for the recipient but also life-changing power for the giver, even if the grace offered is never accepted.

> ### *Roadside Rest*
> **SCRIPTURE FOR MEDITATION**
> In him we have redemption through his blood, the forgiveness of sins, in accordance with the riches of God's grace that he lavished on us with all wisdom and understanding (Ephesians 1:7).

The blessing of being a grace dumper is that grace dumpers live in freedom, above the roiling waters of circumstances. They do not live at the whim of others, dependent upon their actions. Grace dumpers are not reactors but are agents of change in the world around them. They live their lives with a quiet and restrained freedom that belies their true power, the power that comes from their reliance upon the Holy Spirit. Grace dumpers know both who they are and who they are not.

Grace always requires forgiveness, and forgiveness first requires our heartfelt awareness of what we have been forgiven. Apart from that simple truth, we cannot be conduits of grace in the lives of others.

The third *why* of grace is that grace teaches about who we are in Christ.

We are to be bestowers.

We are to be blessers.

We are to be healers.

We are to be helpers.

We are to be binders of the broken and nourishers of the needy.

Grace is given to the humble, and we serve in humble submission to the God who has so abundantly lavished His grace upon us. Philippians 2:3–5 shows us a picture of this humble submission: "Do nothing out of selfish ambition or vain conceit, but in humility consider others better than yourselves. Each of you should look not only to your own interests, but also to the interests of others. Your attitude should be the same as that of Christ Jesus."

> "Grace is given to heal the spiritually sick, not to decorate spiritual heroes."
>
> MARTIN LUTHER

As we learn to swap our thimbles for Mack trucks and learn to lavish grace upon those around us, we become more like Christ, who poured love upon those around Him when they deserved recrimination, who poured compassion upon a world that deserved judgment, and poured out grace upon a world that deserved no less than hell.

When Grace Says No: Grace and Boundaries

Not long after learning that her father had molested her daughter, my friend confronted her dad about his sin, offering him her forgiveness but requiring him to seek counseling and assessment by the courts for the consequences of his actions. He was unrepentant and chose, instead, to further fracture his family by denying his actions. The family healing and accountability that my friend hoped and prayed for didn't come right away. The repentance and remorse she had hoped for from her father has still not come and may never come, but she poured out her grace through forgiveness, nonetheless. She also drew clear boundaries of protection around her daughter and allowed her father to pay the consequences of his sinful, immoral, and illegal actions.

Grace does not mean an abandonment of boundaries and consequences. Sometimes the most loving actions we can take on behalf of our loved ones are the most painful because they involve boundaries and consequences. But God's grace toward us never means looking the other way, ignoring sin. It never involves the abandonment of consequences and allowing pain at the expense of others. I speak as a mother of a prodigal—a broken mom who had the dubious privilege of making the acquaintance of a bail bondsman named Smitty and whose honor it has been to hold other weeping mothers in my arms. For my son, Nathan, consequences, under the direction and power of the Holy Spirit, brought perspective and eventual wisdom that nothing else could have brought.

Family healing and reconciliation didn't come right away for my friend. But spiritual reconciliation with God and earthly reconciliation with family would have been impossible for my friend's father had someone not confronted him with his sin and all of its horrific implications.

Sometimes grace wears the grief-stricken face of accountability, and perhaps that is when it does its most loving work. But it is in those moments when we must carefully guard our hearts, check our motives, and move at the clear direction of the Spirit of God.

Looking Like Papa: Grace and the Character of God

It's impossible to think about the character of God without thinking about grace. And it needs to be that way with us, too. Grace should be woven through the very fabric of our lives. Forgiveness, blessing, hope, affirmation, encouragement, woven through the words that we speak, the tone that we choose, the expression that we reflect, the actions that we portray. Even in the most mundane of moments, the moments that measure the character of who we really are.

When we discover that two prescriptions have run out, and the caregiver is late, and Dad is refusing to take the meds we do have.

When Mom is sick in the middle of the night, and we know we're heading out to the ER again.

When the doctor isn't returning our calls, we haven't slept through the night in four months, and there's no hope for respite.

When our spouse informs us that the alternator is going out on the car, and we won't be able to use the van to drive our parents to the doctor, and we don't know how we'll load a wheelchair into the trunk of our Mazda.

When we haven't heard from our kids in seven weeks and from anyone at church forever, and we're pretty sure that the mailman and our sick husband are the only people who know we're alive anymore.

When we've been put on hold for the sixth time by the mail-order prescription company, after having our call transferred three times and disconnected twice.

It's in those moments that we're asked to measure our maturity—to look in the mirror and to see how much we resemble our Father.

Do we speak words of grace?

Do our eyes and tone reflect a spirit of grace?

Do we forgive with grace?

Do we see others with the eyes of grace?

Do we lavish grace or measure it in thimbles?

My prayer is to become more like a young African American mother. That in the jostle and tumble of life, when I am insulted and affronted, I will stand unflinchingly in the knowledge of who I am and offer life and redemption. That the face of grace I portray to the world would be the face of my Father reflected in my own.

Prayer

Father God, you have dumped your grace over my life again and again, and I'm the recipient of your forgiveness and abundant blessing in so many ways. Make me a conduit of blessing in the lives of others. May I have a heart that beats with a desire to pass on the same grace that I've received. Give me wisdom and discernment to speak words of grace. May my tone and the things that I communicate even nonverbally communicate grace. Give me eyes of grace that allow me to see others as you see them—through the righteousness of Jesus. Make me a bestower, a blesser, a healer, a helper, a binder of the broken and wounded. In Jesus' precious name, amen.

Meditation and Personal Application Questions

1. How would you have responded to a public insult like the one the young mother at the beginning of the chapter received? With words of grace? What kind of response typically comes to your mind when you're "ambushed" by rudeness and disrespect?
2. Grace and forgiveness are closely linked. What distinguishing aspects do they seem to have biblically?
3. Do you consider yourself to be someone who measures out grace in Mack truckloads or thimbles? Does your measure vary in certain types of situations? With certain people?
4. Where have you struggled most with grace in the daily aspects of your caregiving?
5. Read John 17. This is Jesus' final prayer before His crucifixion. What elements of grace poured out on mankind do you see represented in His life in this final prayer?

Scripture for Further Meditation

2 Corinthians 8:7
Titus 2:11–12
2 Peter 3:18

Resources

See appendix 14, "Grace and Becoming an Elder."

As the Father has loved me, so have I loved you.
Now remain in my love.
If you obey my commands, you will remain in my love,
just as I have obeyed my Father's commands and
remain in his love.
I have told you this
so that my joy may be in you and that your joy
may be complete.
My command is this: Love each other as I have loved you.

JOHN 15:9-12

Chapter Nine

Caregiving and Patching Our Pumps

CULTIVATING A SPIRIT OF JOY

"Caregiving has taught me to understand that joy isn't measured by what I see today but by what I see in the total equation of eternity. People who understand art and want to view a great masterpiece don't stand with their noses pressed to the canvas. They stand at a distance and view the work in its entirety. Joy is like that. I can see the purpose and the beauty in the tiny speck of my caregiving when I stand back and consider that I'm a dab of color somewhere in God's magnificent design."

Steve

My friend Jim had me more than a little scared.

Jim was one of those guys who had always gotten more done by ten o'clock in the morning than I had done by the time I had dropped into bed at night. A dedicated husband and father of seven, he was a hard worker. But lately he hadn't been himself.

Over the past few months, Jim had been sidelined with episodes of dizziness, disorientation, and exhaustion so overwhelming, he would drop to his knees. He had visited doctor after doctor and gotten a litany of diagnoses from inner ear problems to stress. They had even run a few tests, but no one could find anything wrong.

Jim knew I had experienced similar medical frustrations. I had visited doctors regularly for over a year, complaining of sounds in my ears, dizziness, loss of equilibrium, and nausea. Nobody seemed too concerned, so I had told myself not to be concerned either, until the day my brain sort of melted down and I found myself unable to stand, walk, see, or recall my own middle name.

One brain lesion and eight months later, I had regained enough of my brain cells to remember how to make a sandwich and to pretend that I could never be trusted in a kitchen again (not that I had ever been trusted anyway). But my experience had taught me how to be a good medical advocate, ask good questions, and be tenacious with doctors when my spirit told me something was truly wrong.

And my spirit told me something was truly wrong with Jim. His symptoms were alarming and getting worse fast. I also knew a lot of great docs well enough to pull some strings. I contacted the best cardiologist I knew and helped make connections that assured Jim an appointment ASAP.

The doctor ran every test in the book with no remarkable results—except one—the last one. A trans-esophageal echocardiogram revealed that Jim had a small hole in the back of his heart. During open-heart surgery, the doctors discovered that the picture was actually far more grim. The hole was almost the size of a fifty-cent piece, and the surrounding tissue was the consistency of Swiss cheese. The lifeblood that was supposed to be sustaining Jim was literally draining from his body. The doctor told him that if the hole had been left unattended, he would have died in less than two weeks. He would have dropped to his knees and never gotten up again.

There are a lot of certainties and uncertainties in life. But one thing is for certain about the way our Creator designed our bodies. Once our blood stops flowing, we are done for.

The Pulsating Flow: Joy

Oswald Chambers has said, "Joy is the nature of God in my blood." It courses through us with the beat of our hearts as naturally as our breathing. It is not something we manufacture or produce but is part of who God created us to be as image bearers. It's infused within our nature and is a foundational confidence that God is in control, regardless of what we see or experience. It is the assurance of knowing that after we've done all we can do, we can rest, knowing God is fully responsible for the outcome.

> "Biblical joy consists of the deep and abiding confidence that all is well, regardless of circumstances or difficulty."
>
> JOHN MACARTHUR, *Joy and Godliness: The Epistle of Joy*

As caregivers, this truth can be our greatest struggle: resting in the confidence that a good and loving God is in control, regardless of what we see or experience, regardless of what we know our loved one is experiencing.

So where do we find joy in the middle of pain and suffering, fatigue, and conflicting priorities? Where do we find a spiritual confidence that all can be truly well, in spite of a physical and emotional world locked in turmoil and anguish?

Flinging Open the Door: When Trials Come Knocking

We often sing a chorus at our church with lyrics taken from the text of James 1:2: "Consider it pure joy, my brothers, whenever you face trials of many kinds, because you know that the testing of your faith develops perseverance. Perseverance must finish its work so that you may be mature and complete, not lacking anything." The chorus speaks of flinging open the door of our heart when the trials of life come knocking. These words have rocked me to my core because most of my life I've been a door slammer.

The days when it's hardest for me to get the words out are the days when David is leading worship, his face lifted in adoration to God, his smile lighting the auditorium, his hands raised. A good decade younger than I, David, with his exuberance, draws you into worship, so you have to be looking hard to notice the tremor in his left hand—the tremor from his Parkinson's disease.

David is a walking, living, breathing picture of joy. He is not a perfect man, but a man who has confidence that all is well, despite his circumstances. He has opened the door to his trial and welcomed it. Does he enjoy Parkinson's? No. Does he want to be healed? Yes. But he has learned the purpose of trials, revealed in James 1:2–4. His passion, above all things, is to be mature and complete, and in that passion, he has made the choice to *consider*, to *count*, and *regard* his trial to be pure joy. David has made a conscious act of will and volition: the choice of his attitude, with a pure motive and intent. He has chosen to let joy course through his veins as his very lifeblood as daily he longs for the maturity promised in James.

> ### Roadside Rest
>
> **SCRIPTURE FOR MEDITATION**
>
> No discipline seems pleasant at the time, but painful. Later on, however, it produces a harvest of righteousness and peace for those who have been trained by it (Hebrews 12:11).

David has flung open the door to his trial. Even in the moments when he weeps and grieves. Even in the moments of struggle. Joy has given him the power to face what lies ahead because David knows what's on the other side of the door.

Getting a Grip on the Knob: Understanding the Big Picture

The secret to the source of our joy is wrapped up in understanding the spiritual payoff. We're promised that trials are just the means to the end, and the end is what redemption has been about from the beginning: God promises to conform us to the image of

His Son. It's through the challenge of trials that we develop the fruit of the Spirit: love, joy, peace, patience, kindness, goodness, faithfulness, gentleness, and self-control, spoken of in Galatians 5:22. As we choose to trust His commitment to work all things for our good, we can choose an attitude of joy. With the promise of our spiritual maturity at stake, we can grab the knob and fling open the door.

Imagine the reality of the promise we're given: the character of Christ revealed in and through us. It's the promise that keeps us pressing forward in the struggle.

When the Door Gets Stuck: Conditions of Joy

But joy doesn't flow automatically. My friend David would tell you that, as he and his wife, Colleen, leave their kids behind and head out the door to consult another Parkinson's specialist. My friend Cindy would tell you that as she bundles her daughter Alicia off for her fortieth brain surgery and leaves her other three children and husband behind. But John 15:9–12 lays down conditions to the free flow of joy in our lives.

> But abiding in Jesus, you come into contact with His infinite love; its fire begins to burn within your heart; you see the beauty of love; you learn to look upon loving and serving and serving your fellow man as the highest privilege a disciple of Jesus can have.
>
> ANDREW MURRAY,
> *The True Vine*

As the Father has loved me, so have I loved you. Now remain in my love. If you obey my commands, you will remain in my love, just as I have obeyed my Father's commands and remain in his love. I have told you this so that my joy may be in you and that your joy may be complete. My command is this: Love each other as I have loved you.

The flow of joy can be blocked, first of all, by not abiding in Christ. Abiding means that we draw our strength from Christ—that we are rooted in Him. Abiding signifies a constant union and connection. This doesn't come naturally—especially for the caregiver. Life pulls at us from a thousand different directions. The tyranny of the urgent. The crush of the crisis. The press of priorities. They all vie to tear us away from our place of abiding.

Yet the voice of Christ calls us to moment-by-moment fellowship. First Thessalonians 5:16–18 states it simply: "Be joyful always; pray continually; give thanks in all circumstances, for this is God's will for you in Christ Jesus."

> Finding the joy in caregiving has to do with setting new priorities, learning to value little steps, letting go of old ideas and expectations, and accepting life as it unfolds. Even in some of our darkest moments, joy surfaced because I allowed it to happen. And it happened on what can only be described as profound levels.
>
> BEVERLY BIGTREE MURPHY,
> "Where Is the Joy in
> Alzheimer's Caregiving?"

Our joy can be blocked, secondly, by disobedience to God's commands as revealed in His Word. The potential for sin is as far-reaching as the human heart. But truth be told, we all struggle with our blind spots—the sinful areas of our lives we've learned to sweep under the rug with justified resentment and disappointment. These can often become the "sins that easily beset us"—the things that take hold of our hearts and cling to them like scum on the shower walls.

Justified resentment is a trap for caregivers because as servers, we're prone to slip into the mental attitude of martyrdom. It's easy to think we deserve to be treated better by _____ (fill in the blank with the relative/health professional/church member/fellow employee/neighbor/friend), who annoys us the most. It's easy to think we're allowed to indulge in a little gossip, a little sputtering, a little backlash, a little *attitude* now and then.

But we're not.

We're asked to look at the big picture—our spiritual maturity and ultimate transformation into Jesus' image. We're to look at the joy laid before us—to love as Jesus loved.

Our joy can be blocked, finally, by our lack of love for others. This truth goes directly to the heart of the double-love command. Christ's love is not a conceptual expression. It's a practical expression of sacrifice and service. Our love for others is a conduit for God's joy in our lives.

In caregiving, our joy is a conduit to our own spiritual growth. It's the pipe driven deeply into the well of God's love. It's the means through which His blessing bubbles to the surface and provides refreshment in our lives and in the lives of others.

The Sacred Paradox: Joy in Sorrow

Scripture makes it clear in passage after passage that a relationship exists between joy and sorrow. Over and over again, the two are linked.

Hebrews 12:2–3:	Let us fix our eyes on Jesus, the author and perfecter of our faith, who for the joy set before him endured the cross, scorning its shame, and sat down at the right hand of the throne of God. Consider him who endured such opposition from sinful men, so that you will not grow weary and lose heart.
John 16:20	I tell you the truth, you will weep and mourn while the world rejoices. You will grieve, but your grief will turn to joy.
Romans 5:3–4	Not only so, but we also rejoice in our sufferings, because we know that suffering

produces perseverance; perseverance, character; and character, hope.

2 Corinthians 7:4 I have great confidence in you; I take great
pride in you. I am greatly encouraged; in all
our troubles my joy knows no bounds.

In fact, Scripture indicates clearly that sorrow increases our joy
as our character is shaped into Christ's image. In spite of our feelings or our circumstances, we can know true joy. Our joy is refined
in our sorrow, as we taste the sweetness and sufficiency of God in
deeper and more meaningful ways.

When Dan and I watched his father slip into respiratory failure,
we knew it would be agonizing to walk beside Norman through the
valley of the shadow of death. But we also knew it would be beautiful. We would experience the most intimate moments of Norman's
journey, as he passed from this life to the next. Had we not walked
through that time, we would never have shared those intimacies
with Norman or known God's sufficiency in those moments. Our
joy can be refined in sorrow. God intended sorrow to be a pathway
to His heart if we choose to follow where it leads.

The Heart of the Matter:
The Wonder-Working Power of the Blood

Recently I saw my good friend Jim Conway, whose heart is
patched and strong and pumping to beat the band. His wife, Shirley, on his arm, he flew through the door of a Christian bookstore
where I was doing a signing so we could catch up on our kids and
life and the goodness of God.

Jim is living, breathing proof that there's wonder-working
power in the blood.

It's coursing through his veins, sustaining him, keeping him
on his feet, giving him fuel for the next breath. Jim is a picture of
joy—a man with a patched pump, imperfect, but pressing on to

maturity, just like my friend David. They are both men who have taught me what living, breathing joy looks like—someone whose eyes are so fixed on Jesus that they see all the way down the road to the end.

Meditation and Personal Application Questions

1. Where have you found joy linked to sorrow in your caregiving? How did you grow through these experiences?
2. Have you known someone like Dave who has pressed on toward maturity in the difficult experiences in life? What was the source of that person's strength?
3. Evaluate the Scriptures below regarding resting and remaining and apply them to your own experiences. How are they speaking to your heart?
4. Has your grief ever turned to joy (John 16:20)? In what ways, and how was this accomplished? Or do you struggle to believe this is possible?

Scripture for Further Meditation

Remaining:	John 15:7–8
	1 John 2:27
Resting:	Deuteronomy 33:12

When Jesus saw his mother there,
and the disciple whom he loved standing nearby,
he said to his mother,
"Dear woman, here is your son," and to the disciple,
"Here is your mother."
From that time on, this disciple took her into his home.

JOHN 19:26–27

Chapter Ten

Surviving the Landing

JESUS' LESSONS FOR LONG-HAUL CAREGIVING

"When my husband and I took our son Vernon, who had multiple sclerosis, and his two sons, who were five and eight, into our home, my husband Louie was well into his seventies. But Louie had the strength of a thirty-year-old and could lift Vernon like he was a child, and we knew we were committed to doing this together. Then on a trip to Kentucky, at a family gathering, my husband's intestines burst, and he was gone.

"Everyone told me I couldn't do it myself—that an older woman barely five feet tall and losing her sight couldn't raise two teenage boys and care for her son dying of MS. But I was determined to try. I'm a lot like Shadrach, Meshach, and Abednego. God can put me to the test, but I'm still going to trust Him.

"My family got me the best equipment available and supported me in every way they could. I took care of Vernon in my home until he died. I was able to take him to church with me until that final week. I can't say it wasn't hard, but I can say God's grace is sufficient.

"On the days when my son was lying on the ground and I didn't know how I'd get him up, I learned to take a breath and pray, 'God, I need your help.' He was always there. I remember that every time I'm tempted to have a pity party."

Viva

I had barely settled myself into the plush wingback chair before the television talk-show host leaned forward and touched my arm.

"My father was diagnosed with Alzheimer's at the age of fifty-two. We took care of him for twelve years. When I read the stories in your book, they went off like gunshots in my heart because they were my stories, too. Those years were precious, but they were tough.

"We've got to find ways to take better care of our caregivers. They're a fragile resource, and without them, our loved ones are at risk. We've got to create ways to help families for the long haul."

For many caregivers, the journey is a long haul. In the years ahead, it's predicted that some adults may spend more years caring for their parents than they'll spend caring for their children. And as demographics shift as the elderly live longer and families continue to fragment with divorce, the ratio of caregivers to those needing care will continue to diminish.

Roadside Realities

The average caregiver provides care for a loved one for 4.3 years.

The National Alliance for Caregivers

Long-Haul Care: Viva's Story

No one knows the secret of long-haul caregiving better than my friend Viva. She began at the age of five, when her father lost the farm and her siblings were split up. Hard work and looking out for others were always second nature to Viva. So years later, when her son with multiple sclerosis lost his wife and mother of his two young boys, the only thing Viva knew was to strap herself to Jesus and take the first step. Like a child in a three-legged race, she gave way to the pull of a stride that she couldn't control and stepped into the rhythm of the pace. She ignored the laws of physics that clearly demonstrated that a pint-sized elderly woman couldn't care for the needs of a wheelchair-bound man. She simply did it without fanfare over the months as her son's body failed him, until he passed away. Then she pressed on, raising her two grandsons.

Viva didn't seem to know any other way to do it than to just do it, to rest in the Lord along the way. But she never paid much attention to the "couldn'ts" of life. She was too busy concentrating on what needed to be done.

You may know a Viva. You may even be one—a spirited saint of God who finds new mercies and energy for the task every morning. But chances are you're like most of us. You struggle. You feel your knees go weak under the weight of discouragement, fatigue, isolation. At times you may feel you have nowhere to turn and that you've been abandoned in the journey. You may look at Viva's example and wonder how she managed to pull herself out of bed every morning.

The secret to her marathon success was simple. She learned early on not to depend upon herself. She knew her source of strength was found in God and His limitless supply. She knew, more than anyone, that her stride was too short, her endurance too limited. She knew that her sufficiency was in her dependency upon God to meet her needs and the needs of her son and grandsons.

The Pace-Setter: Jesus the Caregiver

Viva could be defined as a marathon caregiver. And the secret to her success was understanding the principles that emanated from the heart of Jesus and characterized His caregiving ministry. While Christ came to embody the plan of redemption for mankind, He also came as a caregiver. He healed and helped. He tended and ministered. He consoled and comforted. Our ultimate example for caregiving can be found in Jesus Christ. He healed not only bodies but souls, and the touch of His hands reached beyond the temporal to the eternal. In His earthly ministry, as He became one with humanity, He cared for the needs of countless sick and needy persons who pressed Him from every side

As a caregiver, Jesus demonstrated the core principles from which we can draw strength for our caregiving journeys.

Jesus drew His strength from knowing who He was as God's Son.

Jesus, as the eternal, holy Son of God, drew His source of strength from the Holy Spirit and from His relationship with His heavenly Father. He lived in constant communion with God through the ministry of the Holy Spirit, and He had the inexhaustible resources of God at His disposal.

Yet He was susceptible to weariness and discouragement, grief and pain. He knew the press of the crowds and the desire to flee from the weight of crushing responsibilities. But the source of His sufficiency was His identity: God the Son.

> Then Jesus declared, "I am the bread of life. He who comes to me will never go hungry, and he who believes in me will never be thirsty. But as I told you, you have seen me and still you do not believe. All that the Father gives me will come to me, and whoever comes to me I will never drive away. For I have come down from heaven not to do my will but to do the will of him who sent me" (John 6:35–38).

Jesus knew that His identity, His sufficiency, and His destiny were rooted in the character of God the Father. His intimacy with the Father was the foundation for every action, every thought, every conversation, every motive.

Our ultimate source of strength is in our identity as God's children—in knowing that His inexhaustible riches are at our disposal, that He yearns to be in communion with us and to know our deepest needs and longings, and that He is the source of our sufficiency.

Jesus spent frequent time alone in prayer.

In the past seven years, I can count on one hand the number of times I've been alone in my home overnight. Yet recently, just hours after I had received crushing personal news, I faced three days of solitude in my house.

I was home, devastated and broken, alone with God.

It was gut-wrenching, and it was glorious.

Isabel Burton wrote, "I saw the desert, it grew upon me. There are times when I have sorrows, that I hunger and thirst for it."[1] In my days of struggle, I needed to be alone. I needed to lean deeply upon God's strength and cry out to Him for wisdom, knowing there would be difficult days ahead.

Jesus, too, refreshed His spirit by drawing aside from the crowds to press in to the heart of the Father. He knew His sufficiency in facing the rejection of His ministry and the agony of His death would come from His communion with the Father.

Matthew 14:13	"[Jesus] withdrew by boat privately to a solitary place…"
Matthew 14:23	"After he had dismissed them, he went up on a mountainside by himself to pray."
Mark 1:35	"Very early in the morning, while it was still dark, Jesus got up, left the house and went off to a solitary place, where he prayed."
Luke 4:42	"At daybreak Jesus went out to a solitary place."

---

1. Isabel Burton, *The Inner Life of Syria, Palestine, and the Holy Land,* as quoted in *Beauty by the Book* by Nancy Stafford (Sisters, Oregon: Multnomah, 2002), 130.

Luke 5:16	"But Jesus often withdrew to lonely places and prayed."
Luke 6:12	"One of those days Jesus went out to a mountainside to pray, and spent the night praying to God."
Luke 11:1	"One day Jesus was praying in a certain place."

Jesus' private prayer life provided the power that pulsated through His ministry in the same way His lifeblood coursed through His veins. He poured out in ministry to others, then drew away, always to spend time in intimate communion with His Father.

When was the last time you were alone with God? When was the last time you ran away from the crowds for much-needed rest— to sleep, to watch a sunset, to lay your head upon the heart of God and pour out your longings? These desert experiences aren't optional; they're the food of our souls. Thomas Merton understood the need for desert sustenance: "It is in deep solitude that I find the gentleness with which I can truly love my brothers... Solitude and silence teach me to love my brothers for what they are, not for what they say."[2]

Jesus spent time with His closest friends in prayer.

As well as drawing aside for private times of prayer, Jesus often took His disciples and most intimate companions with Him.

| Matthew 17:1 | "After six days Jesus took with him Peter, James and John the brother of James, and led them up a high mountain by themselves." |
| Luke 9:18 | "Once when Jesus was praying in private and his disciples were with him..." |

---

2. Thomas Merton, *The Sign of Jonas* (New York: Harcourt, Brace & Co., 1953), 261.

Luke 9:28   "About eight days after Jesus said this, he
                   took Peter, John and James with him and
                   went up onto a mountain to pray."

Luke 11:1ff.   "One day Jesus was praying in a certain
                   place. When he finished, one of his disciples
                   said to him, 'Lord, teach us to pray, just as
                   John taught his disciples.'"

Prayer was not just a time of communion with His Father, it was a time of intimacy with those who were dearest to Him. Jesus could have chosen to keep His prayer time a private time of seclusion, but instead He chose to invite others in.

We, too, need the communion and accountability of friends and loved ones. It feeds my soul to be able to look into the eyes of Darice and Cami, dear prayer partners. Just knowing they understand my struggles can feed my soul. As caregivers, we see that our prayer partners are not a luxury; they are a necessity.

> In order to be united to God, you must participate in His infinite stillness . . . Your spirit can never arrive in divine union or become one with God until you have been established in His rest and purity.
>
> MADAM GUYON

Jesus publicly gave thanks and reflected glory back to God.

In the gospel accounts where Jesus fed the crowds that followed Him, we see Him publicly expressing thanks for what God had provided.

Matthew 14:19   "Taking the five loaves and the two fish and
                   looking up to heaven, he gave thanks and
                   broke the loaves."

| Matthew 15:36 | "Then he took the seven loaves and the fish, and when he had given thanks, he broke them and gave them to the disciples…" |
| Mark 6:41 | "Taking the five loaves and the two fish and looking up to heaven, he gave thanks and broke the loaves." |

In spite of the drain of a long and wearying day, Jesus chose to deliver a public prayer before the crowds that directed thanks to God. He used circumstance after circumstance to draw people's attention to the Father's goodness and provision.

In Jesus' first recorded conversation in Scripture—a dialogue with Satan during the temptation in the desert—Jesus claims the sufficiency of God's nature and character: "Jesus answered, 'It is written: "Man does not live on bread alone, but on every word that comes from the mouth of God"'" (Matthew 4:4).

Jesus' nature is to respond to rebuke, criticism, lies, doubt, and the everyday circumstances of life by glorifying God.

As I talk about the circumstances of my life to others, I can choose the truth to reflect in my conversation. I can complain about my circumstances and imply that God has given me a raw deal; I can draw attention to myself and make *me* the central attraction; or I can give glory to God and reflect praise and confidence in Him.

Jesus knew His confidence was in God, and He faced crisis with calm assurance.

Again, in Jesus' first encounter with Satan in the desert in the book of Matthew, His temptation to give up and give in to an easier, self-serving path was met with quiet confidence. Jesus knew who He was and the source of His power. He met each temptation with the truth of Scripture and moved confidently on.

When Jesus stood before Pilate (John 18:33–37), He met His inquisitor's questions with authority, yet without arrogance.

> Pilate then went back inside the palace, summoned Jesus and asked him, "Are you the king of the Jews?"
>
> "Is that your own idea," Jesus asked, "or did others talk to you about me?"
>
> "Am I a Jew?" Pilate replied. "It was your people and your chief priests who handed you over to me. What is it you have done?"
>
> Jesus said, "My kingdom is not of this world. If it were, my servants would fight to prevent my arrest by the Jews. But now my kingdom is from another place."
>
> "You are a king, then!" said Pilate.
>
> Jesus answered, "You are right in saying I am a king. In fact, for this reason I was born, and for this I came into the world, to testify to the truth. Everyone on the side of truth listens to me."

When crisis came, Jesus didn't panic. He didn't grandstand. He didn't pout. He didn't manipulate. He didn't accuse. He stood confidently in His identity as the Son of God and spoke the truth.

I spent the first five years of my caregiving with my hair on fire. Talk to anyone who shared an office with me, and they'll verify my words. Everything in my caregiving life was a crisis. I recently summarized a few highlights to an editor and realized at the end that if I had slid an offering plate across the table, he would probably have thrown his wallet in. But even though the circumstances were mind-boggling, I chose to live my life in a constant state of quasi-panic, as an addicted adrenaline junkie. My tone, attitude, and actions communicated that God was losing His grip on the world.

I was still working on learning the truth of Isaiah 32:17: "The fruit of righteousness will be peace; the effect of righteousness will be quietness and confidence forever."

Jesus delegated to others when He didn't have to.

One interesting element of Jesus' interaction with the disciples was that He delegated when He simply could have done everything himself. He had the power to perform any kind of miracle necessary to accomplish any kind of results. Yet in the feeding of the masses of people that followed Him, He delegated responsibility to the disciples.

We can only assume that this was because both the disciples and the crowds tagging along had something to gain from the experience. Certainly with a simple thought from Jesus, individual Galilean goodie bags could have appeared in everyone's hands, complete with loaves, fishes, and Mt. Olive bottled water. But instead, Jesus allowed the disciples to be involved in the blessing of caring for the crowd. "You give them something to eat," was His response (Mark 6:37). But He had something up His sleeve—an opportunity for them to be involved in a miracle and to be blessed in the process.

I have to admit that I'm often reluctant to delegate because I'm living on the edge of the moment. But delegation can be a gift to those around us. My friend Amanda appreciated the opportunity to bring her children by to visit "Grandpa and Grandma Burke." And my parents loved the opportunity to have four small children in the house. Amanda loves to cook for me, and has helped me with this responsibility. I know Darice and Rachel and Paul have also been available to help with respite care when they were needed.

Roadside Assistance

Take a few minutes every month to create a list of tasks you can delegate to others to do for you: lawn and garden chores, shopping, gift buying, meal preparation, house cleaning, purchasing stamps, cleaning a closet, etc. Then keep the list handy for when friends ask what they can do to help.

Jesus grieved the losses of those He loved with an eternal perspective.

When Jesus heard that John the Baptist had been killed, He "withdrew by boat privately to a solitary place" (Matthew 14:13). Even the Son of God, who knew the scope of eternity from beginning to end, was impacted by the loss of someone He loved and took time to be by himself.

When Jesus was called to come and heal Lazarus, who had died before He arrived, again He wept, knowing fully that He was going to raise Him from the dead. Yet His tears were for those who were grieving for the one they loved. In John 11:32–35, we read,

> When Mary reached the place where Jesus was and saw him, she fell at his feet and said, "Lord, if you had been here, my brother would not have died."
>
> When Jesus saw her weeping, and the Jews who had come along with her also weeping, he was deeply moved in spirit and troubled. "Where have you laid him?" he asked.
>
> "Come and see, Lord," they replied.
>
> Jesus wept.

Jesus recognized the depth of their grief and mourned with them, even though He carried the perspective of eternity in His soul. He knew the place of loss and suffering in the lives of those who care for the sick.

Jesus knew the place of grief, and He acknowledged it. As caregivers, we face constant grief, not just the grief of death. As I care for a mother with Alzheimer's, I face the daily grief of my mother's losses. I face the grief of watching my father mourn his own losses as his wife physically and mentally dissipates before his eyes.

We grieve for our own losses and for the things we cannot do and the pain we cannot heal. Yet our grief is grief with an eternal perspective. We do not grieve without hope. We grieve with a glorious knowledge that God has written an end to our stories that promises redemption and a future beyond what we can see here and now.

The Three-Legged Race:
Strapping Yourself In

It would take volumes to exhaust the riches of the life of Jesus Christ as it applies to our caregiving journeys. But the applications are simple, yet profound.

Do we draw our strength from our intimate connection with God the Father, knowing who we are in Him?

Do we spend frequent time alone with God in prayer?

Do we gain strength from time with friends in prayer?

Do we publicly give thanks and reflect glory back to God?

Knowing our confidence is in God, do we face crisis with calm assurance?

Do we delegate to others so that they can share in the blessings?

Do we grieve our losses with an eternal perspective?

Do we know Jesus intimately, spending time in His presence through time in the Word and meditation?

Back to Viva:
Strapping Yourself In and Taking the Plunge

I called my friend Viva the other day. She remarried ten years ago at the age of seventy-seven and still sounded like a newlywed on the phone. Her macular degeneration has taken its toll, and she has lost most of her sight. But she told me that only when I came right out and asked.

What came out first in a tumble were all the blessings as she told me about her most recent birthday. On the spur of the moment,

Viva had celebrated in a most surprising way by doing something she had always wanted to do.

She and several family members had been invited to the local airport to watch her granddaughter Shannon sky-dive from an airplane. But to Viva, the opportunity seemed to be too great to pass by. With the wind in her hair and a smile on her face, she decided to take the leap herself, if someone else was willing to pay. She called her grandsons, giving them just enough time to watch her launch herself from an airplane, at the age of eighty-six, strapped securely to a professional tandem parachute jumper.

Viva didn't seem to mind the need to relinquish control of her body to an unknown person as she hurled herself from an airplane a thousand feet in the air. But then, Viva was a pro who had learned decades ago to strap herself to Jesus and enjoy the ride.

Falling Well: The Art of the Landing

Some of us may fulfill our caregiver roles over a period of several months. Others may still be caring for loved ones at the point of our death. But whatever our situation, our role as a caregiver does not define us. Our image-bearing as a child of God defines us. As caregivers, we may be "in it for the long haul," but as children of God, all we do is for the goal of being conformed to the image of Jesus Christ.

Each day of the journey of our life means relinquishing control as we step out in faith and strap ourselves to God for the ride. Someone else has paid the way for us, and it's our job to settle back and enjoy the slap of the wind in our face as we hurtle in a graceful freefall that will land us safely where He intended us to land.

In His arms.

Prayer

Dearest Father, there are days when I feel defeated and abandoned, overwhelmed and oppressed. There are days when I fear what is ahead and regret what lies behind. There are days when I feel that I have failed in all that I have done.

Help me to see that even in those days you are producing something of value for eternity—something that can come only through your power and your strength, for your strength is made perfect in my weakness. You ask only that I believe in you and trust in you for the moments that lie ahead. You ask me to believe that you are fulfilling your purposes, in spite of what I see in the circumstances around me. Forgive me when I doubt. Give me the grace to believe what I cannot see and remember that I'm being shaped when I'm in the crucible.

I believe, Lord. Help my unbelief. May I surrender my heart to yours, trusting you for the glorious, eternal outcome that is even now being revealed, moment by moment.

Meditation and Personal Application Questions

1. Where do you stand in your relationship with Jesus Christ? Are you confident that you're a child of God, having asked for forgiveness of sins and to accept Christ as Savior? In what ways have you grown in your faith recently?

2. What friend(s) do you enjoy praying with or do you feel you might be comfortable praying with? Set a goal of two friends you would like to contact to ask to pray with/for you.

3. Write out a list of jobs that you could delegate to others, and then pray over that list. Ask God to direct you to

specific people who might be able to help unburden you in specific areas of your life.

4. What have you grieved this past year? Scripture tells us that Jesus carries our griefs and sorrows. Specifically name those griefs as you pray, and ask Christ to bear them for you.

5. Read through Psalm 42. Reflect on how this psalm relates to our grieving.

Scripture for Further Meditation

1 John 3:21
Romans 12:3
John 17

You used to walk in these ways, in the life you once lived.
But now you must rid yourselves of all such things as these:
anger, rage, malice, slander, and filthy language from your lips.
Do not lie to each other,
since you have taken off your old self
with its practices and have put on the new self,
which is being renewed in knowledge in the
image of its Creator.

COLOSSIANS 3:7–10

Chapter Eleven

Epilogue

THE GIFT OF GROWING UP

"This is the gut-spilling part. The part where I have to tell you how fearful I was of letting God change me. How fearful I was of having to exchange my self-centered heart for the heart of a true caregiver. And how fearful I was of having to do the difficult work of growing up spiritually and emotionally or else being stuck forever as a spiritual brat.

"For years I didn't want to change because I was mad, and I thought I had good reasons.

"But what I really had was my own selfish ambition. What God gave me in exchange for my sin and my crummy attitude was forgiveness and himself. And then the unexpected—the gift of slowly but surely growing up."

Shelly

It will be easiest if I just begin with the plain truth. For most of my life I've been a spiritual brat. Immaturity can look pretty ugly on an adult. But I've found we can become pretty practiced at slathering our sins with a thin coating of self-delusion.

Before Norman, my father-in-law, came to live with us almost eight years ago, I was a generational bigot. I looked down my nose at the elderly in a patronizing manner, mostly because I didn't understand them and they were different from me, and I believed that in areas where we were different, I was superior. I think most bigots are pretty much like that.

Norman had a strict preference for Pepsodent toothpaste that came from the dollar store, and he was a stickler for checking the price sticker to make sure it was bright green and read "ninety-six cents." On occasions when I purchased his toothpaste somewhere other than Dollar General, I would guiltily scrape the sticker from the box before giving it to him, but he always knew. His beautiful blue eyes would bore into me before he walked away, silently chiding me for trying to trick a sick old man rather than just have the decency to tell him the truth—Dollar General just wasn't on my regular errand circuit.

There were other ways I condescended to Norman. Like the times I flaunted my Christian liberty in front of him because I believed I had a right to Christian liberty. Then I would slink away and ponder my self-proclaimed "liberty," oblivious to the fact that I'd turned it into a club by denigrating a man's dignity.

And then there were the frustrations of my own father's quirks. Above all things, my father's frugality frustrated me. I was distressed by the fact that Dad bought his canvas deck shoes for two dollars at a secondhand store and stuffed newspaper into the toes to make them fit, then chose to *brag* to people about them. I never understood why it was so important for him to try to negotiate a six-dollar haircut, no matter what it looked like when it was done, or why we couldn't buy the twelve-dollar belt at Meijer instead of heading down the street to a thrift store in search of a cheaper one.

Perhaps my greatest annoyance was that my father was devoted to cheap tissues. If war were ever to break out at my house, it would not be about politics or religion—it would be over the merits of cheap tissues over real Kleenex. At his funeral someday, all of my father's loved ones will be scraping their faces with cheap facial tissue in tribute to him. To Dad, real Kleenex is a waste of money when cheap tissues will do the job just as well. Why pay big money for something you're going to . . . well, blow your nose into?

I laughed long and often about my father-in-law's and my parents' idiosyncrasies. As family members, we had our private jokes, and they were mostly loving and harmless. But then there were the *other* times. The times when I knew I was sharing a story at their expense.

When I was frustrated or just not paying attention, I sinned often—both publicly and privately—in my attitude and my conversation. I would occasionally talk about my relatives' oddities to my friends in tones of superiority or condescension, as though they were toddlers or pets. When I was frustrated, I vented to others. I set myself up as a martyr and basked in attention, then carefully deflected my gaze from the mirror of my soul.

I had the foolish tongue and self-centered heart of a child—until the day I was challenged by a godly pastor to put away childish things and repent. Without the consistent teaching and counseling I received, I would still be wallowing in my sin.

Get Over It: It's Time to Grow Up

I remember as a child lying on my bed, brokenhearted, and weeping for what seemed like hours over unkind and harsh words that had been spoken to me. My heart was truly wounded, and I remember the most heart-rending moment of all: the moment when I realized that the crying would never be enough. I would eventually have to find a way to face life again after the insults. I would have to find a way back into the world, as unkind as it might be, or lie on my bed for the rest of my life until I shriveled up and died.

I spent a lot of my adult life acting like that child—curling up and wishing that the crying would take away the pain. But sooner or later, you have to make a decision to move on. You have to make a decision to change or die where you're lying.

The day Norman moved in with us was the day God gave me the opportunity to change or to die where I was lying. I chose to change, even though in the beginning it was in fits and starts.

Caregiving was God's gift to me—a gift of growing up. My battle involved a few temper tantrums, a clash of wills, and a final, glorious abandonment of my self-centered focus. I came to understand that I had placed self-love first and had never really understood the depth of God's love for me and that it alone could be the sustaining wellspring of my love for others. But as I cared for Norman, for my mother, and for my father, God showed me the depth of that love and His sustaining grace. I learned to release my grip on the attitude of entitlement I had clutched to my heart for so long. I began to learn what it meant to love as Jesus loved—selflessly, relentlessly, sacrificially. As I learned to walk in that love, I slowly began to grow into maturity in Christ. Day by day, my spiritual brat habits and attitudes fell away, and, by God's grace, I came to resemble my Father more and more.

A Renewed Vision: A New Attitude

Shame is an emotion that can either immobilize us or inspire us to change. I'm ashamed of the condescending person I used to be and my sinful pride. But I'm forgiven and free in Christ, and today I have a new attitude. I've gained a new attitude for not only my circumstances but also the people around me. The brat can see only himself in his world. The child of God sees not only the face of his Father, but the face of his Father reflected in everyone else he sees.

As my attitude changed, my vision for those I loved began to change. My annoyances began to fade, and I learned to sit in awe of Norman, my father-in-law, whose gentle and uncomplaining spirit graced my home for almost five years. In spite of his physical and mental illnesses, Norman taught our family about perseverance, about devotion in prayer, about selflessness and a gentle and humble spirit. He was a man who knew how to love God well. I learned to appreciate reverence and humility. I learned to be comfortable with silences and solitude. I learned what it means to pray without ceasing and to be content with little.

In these past two years, my own father, Paul Burke, transformed before my eyes and became my walking, living, breathing hero. My father taught me about selfless service as he poured out his life for my mother, day and night, despite the challenges of her Alzheimer's disease. Even in the night, when my mother needed attending, Dad was reluctant to call me to help. In all the years my father shared our home, I never heard a complaint from Dad's lips. He never demanded anything for himself and always sought ways to contribute, never mentioning his own losses when he moved in with us—his home, his freedom to drive, his privacy, his friends. He consistently and quietly put himself last and modeled Christ as he selflessly stepped aside for the sake of others, again and again.

Even in her descent into Alzheimer's, my mother has been a joy. She has retained her sense of humor and continues to grace our family with laughter and delight. Her bright smile has sustained and fed our spirits. Music has always been her joy, and she still sings with us. I cannot think of my mother without thinking of her sweet alto voice lifted in praise to God beside me at church.

Tonight is a special night. The clock in the living room is chiming ten p.m. Dan is at a meeting, and I'm alone. For the first time in almost eight years, there is no one to help to bed. It's been a year-and-a-half since Norman passed away and my mother and father moved in with us. But tonight they're with my brother, Paul, and his wife, Sheryl, preparing to be moved into a nursing care facility on the other side of the state. My heart is having its own wrestling match of emotions over this new caregiving scenario for Mom and Dad. I've been cast in the role of a caregiver for so many years, I'm not quite certain how to navigate my way back out.

After all, it took me years to grow to love parsnips and appreciate the merits of cheap facial tissue. And I've come to earnestly love incomprehensible conversations at dinnertime. And I can't quite bring myself to pull the spare adult diaper out from under the seat of my car or take the extra nightlights out of the sockets in the spare room. I can't make myself box up the winter clothes and mail them off just yet, although I feel a strange need to send my father his Dutch Rusk and his assortment of jams.

When I began my caregiving journey almost eight years ago, I mistakenly thought I would be giving to those I loved. I was proven to be wrong. Like my friend Mona, I never gave a fraction of what I received. I learned along the way that God always asks us first to open our hands to give before we can receive.

Spiritual transformation in caregiving is about giving what you were never intended to keep—God's unfathomable love—and along the way, discovering that the journey will change you forever in unexpected, soul-bending ways, as you're ambushed by grace.

Prayer

Dear Father God, forgive me for my self-centeredness and the pride that has kept me a spiritual brat. Forgive me for my condescending attitude toward others who are different from me, whether they are the elderly, young people, those of different races or cultures, or those who don't know you. Convict me of my sin of pride and prejudice and forgive me, Father. Work deeply within my heart to reveal these attitudes and change me.

Today I take off the old self and put on the new. My desire is to see my parents and loved ones through your eyes. Give me an appreciation for those things that make us different. Give me a passion for their heart, dear Father. May our hearts be reconciled where there has been separation. May there be healing where there has been woundedness. May there be steps toward communication where there have been silence and separation.

Give me a willing heart to take the first steps toward soul-bending change. Give me wisdom through the power of your Holy Spirit. I ask these things in Jesus' name, amen.

Meditation and Personal Application Questions

1. Do you feel you've been guilty of generational prejudice in your attitudes and actions? How has pride affected the way you view others who are different from you? What specific things do you feel convicted to confess in this area?

2. In what ways have you hung on to childish spiritual attitudes? Where do you need to grow up and into maturity?

3. Specifically list areas of appreciation for your mother and father, mother-in-law and father-in-law, even if those relationships have been broken and painful. How do you believe God views those relationships, and what steps do you feel He would want to be taken toward reconciliation?

4. Read Ephesians 4:12–16. What does this passage say about growing into maturity in Christ? In what ways would you consider yourself a "spiritual brat"?

5. What does Ephesians 4:29–32 say about the characteristics of the mature believer? Pray through this passage and ask the Holy Spirit to impress upon your heart specific areas that might need confession and reconciliation with a loved one.

Scripture for Further Meditation

Leviticus 19:34
Jeremiah 29:11
Ephesians 4:32

Afterword

A number of transitions have come to pass since the manuscript of this book was written. My mother's needs became an increasing priority, and she and my father were moved into an intimate assisted living facility two-and-a-half hours across the state near my brother, Paul, where they shared a room and were cared for lavishly by Paul and his family. Three days ago my mother went home to be with the Lord, surrounded by family as she lay at the side of her devoted husband, Paul Burke.

Even in my mother's death, I found myself ambushed by grace. Her life was a heritage of godliness that reflected a life of loving devotion to her Savior, Jesus Christ.

But my greatest comfort was knowing that the grave is not the end. As believers, we are graced with a hope that is fixed in the eternal love of God. Even in sorrow, we have hope because we personally know the Author of hope, the One who overcame death so that we can know what it means to live in communion with Him and to be ambushed, over and over again, by His amazing grace.

Practical Help for the Caregiver Resource List

Accreditation of Eldercare Facilities

Accreditation Commission for Health Care
919.786.1214

Carescout.com
800.571.1918

National League for Nursing Accrediting Commission
800.669.1656 x 1
www.nlnac.org

Joint Commission on Accreditation of Healthcare Organizations
630.792.5000

National Association for Home Care & Hospice
202.547.7424
www.nahc.org

National Association of State Units on Aging
202.898.2578

Nursing Home Compare Database, service of Medicare
800.633.4227
www.medicare.gov

NursingHomeReports.com

Alzheimer's

Alzheimer's Association
800.272.3900
www.alz.org

Alzheimer's Disease Education and Referral Center
800.438.4380
www.alzheimers.org

Alzheimer's Association Safe Return Program
800.272.3900
www.alz.org/SafeReturn

Area Agency on Aging

Area Agency on Aging in the blue pages of the phone directory under "Guide to Human Services"
www.n4a.org

Care Managers

American Association of Daily Money Managers
877.326.5991
www.aadmm.com

National Association of Professional Geriatric Care Managers
520.881.8008
www.caremanager.org

National Association of Social Workers
800.638.8799
www.socialworkers.org

Communication

Visiting with Elders by Ruth Goodman and Baycrest Public Affairs
Toronto, Ontario, 2006
www.baycrest.org

Creative Caring Resources

www.alzstore.com
Resources for those with Alzheimer's

www.videorespite.com
Resources for those with dementias and chronic illnesses

www.aarp.org/games
Online games

Day Services

Homecare Online
www.nahc.org

National Adult Day Services Association
877.745.1440
www.nadsa.org

Standards and Guidelines for Adult Day Care
www.nadsa.org

In-home support services—the county Department of Human Services in the government listings in the blue pages of the phone directory.

Driving

AARP Driver Safety Course
$10 for an 8-hour refresher taught over 2 days
888.AARP-NOW
www.AARP.org/families/driver_safety

Association for Driver Rehabilitation Specialists
800.290.2344
www.driver-ed.org

National Highway Safety Administration
Booklets on assessing diminishing driving abilities
888-DASH-2-DOT
www.nhtsa.gov

Look in the blue pages of the phone directory for your state Department of Transportation, where assessments for general driving skill, memory, reaction time, and visual acuity may be available upon a doctor's referral.

Health Care

American Stroke Association
www.strokeassociation.org

Mayo Clinic Resources Online
www.mayoclinic.com

National Council on Aging
www.ncoa.org

Parkinson's Disease Foundation
www.pdf.org

Stroke Family Support Network
888.478.7653

Visiting Nurse Associations of America
800.426.2547
www.vnaa.org

Hospice

Partnership for Caring, *Caring Connections*—Resources for end of life and palliative care issues

National Hospice and Palliative Care Organization
800.658.8898
www.nho.org
www.caringinfo.org

Hospice Link
800.331.1620
www.hospiceworld.org

Insurance

The National Insurance Consumer Help
212.346.5500
www. iii.org

National Association of Insurance Commissioners
www.naic.org

Legal Assistance

National Academy of Elder Law Attorneys
520.881.4005
www.naela.org

National Fraud Information Center
800.876.7060
www.fraud.org
Federal Trade Commission 877.382.4357

Nolo Press
Self-help books on legal issues for caregivers and care
recipients
800.728.3555
www.nolo.com

Partnership for Caring/National Hospice
Free state-specific sample forms for durable power of attorney
for health care and living wills
800.989.9455
www.partnershipforcaring.org

Meals on Wheels

Meals on Wheels Association of America
703.548.5558
www.mowaa.org

Medicaid

Medicaid Services
www.cms.hhs.gov

Social Security

www.ssa.gov

Support Services

A Place for Mom
www.aplaceformom.com

About: Senior Living
Web site with diverse resources and links regarding senior living topics
www.about.com Search Senior Living topic

Administration on Aging
www.aoa.gov

Ageless Design
Home modification resources
www.agelessdesign.com

Agenet
www.agenet.com
Solutions for better aging

The Assisted Living Federation of America
List of member facilities that can be searched by state, county, and city
www.alfa.org

Consumers
703.691.8100

The American Association of Homes and Services for the Aging
202.783.2242
www.aahsa.org

CareScout/National Eldercare Referral Systems
800.571.1918

Caring Today: Practical Advice for the Family Caregiver
www.caringtoday.com

Children of Aging Parents
www.caps4caregivers.org

The Consumer Consortium on Assisted Living
703.533.8121
www.ccal.org

Eldercare Locator, U.S. Administration on Aging
800.677.1116
www.eldercare.gov

Faith in Action
www.fiavolunteers.org

Family Caregiver Alliance
www.caregiver.org

Home Care Assistance
www.homecareassistance.com

National Alliance for Caregiving
www.caregiving.org

National Association of Social Workers
www.naswdc.org

National Council on Aging
Free online service for eligibility for benefits for health care,
financial assistance, and legal counseling
www.benefitscheckup.org

National Institute on Aging
800.222.2225
www.nia-nih.gov

Share the Care
Assistance in forming a caregiving support group
www.sharethecare.org

Well Spouse Association
www.wellspouse.org

Taxes

Tax Counseling for the Elderly, sponsored by the Internal
Revenue Service
800.829.1040

The Volunteer Income Tax Assistance Program
800.829.1040

Veterans' Services

Department of Veterans Affairs
800.827.1000
www.va.gov
"Compensation and Benefits" and "Facilities Locator"

Veterans Medical Services
877.222.VETS

Veterans of Foreign Wars Service Hotline
800.VFW.1899
www.vfw.org

Should Your Parent Move In with You?

*O*ne of the most significant decisions you may have to make in your caregiving scenario is whether your parent will move into your home. Before making a decision, consider the following areas of concern. Discuss them with all family members who would be impacted by the decision. Sometimes homecare is best, and sometimes family needs are best served by placing a loved one in assisted living, a retirement community, by bringing care into their own home, or through another creative alternative.

Physical Space

- Is your home large enough to provide privacy for all family members once your parent moves in? Would your parent have his or her own bedroom? Bathroom? Sitting area?
- Are family members resentful or reluctant about giving up what was previously their "personal" space?

Relationships

- Do your spouse and other family members living at home get along with your parent?
- Is your parent anxious or irritable? Depressed? Easily frustrated?
- Are your children mature enough to understand why their grandparent is moving into your home, and are they mature enough to welcome him or her?

- Will you be able to view yourself as a decision-making, in-charge adult and not feel like a child in the presence of your parent?
- Have you resolved any past conflicts with your parent, and do the two of you get along well now?

Adaptability

- Will family members willingly make adjustments?
- Will your parent be willing and able to make the necessary adjustments to your home environment?
- Is your parent frustrated by the tasks of daily life (dressing, organizing mail, meal preparation, etc.)?
- Is your parent comfortable in social environments?
- Is your parent capable of willingly adapting to the culture and environment of your home?
- Are your lifestyle and values compatible with your parent's?
- Will you feel comfortable asking your parent to pitch in with household chores, finances, or childcare, if he or she is able?
- Can he or she grocery shop and assist with simple chores?
- Are you able to proceed with moving your parent into your home without feelings of resentment?

Medical and Health Concerns

- Does your parent have a form of dementia? If so, how will this impact family dynamics?
- Will your parent be safe in your home (locks, stove and oven, falls, etc.)?
- Does your house have wheelchair-accessible entryways and handrails and grab bars by the toilet, bathtub, and shower?
- Does your loved one still drive? How will those limitations impact your family schedule?

- Do you have concerns regarding your parent's reflexes, vision, memory, ability to respond to the unexpected, or ability to find her way if she becomes lost?
- Has your loved one been diagnosed with a disease or medical condition that impacts his daily living?
- Is this medical disease degenerative in nature, posing potential future limitations?
- Is her weight stable? Does she eat balanced meals? Can she be trusted to safely prepare simple meals?
- Is he still capable of independent, good hygiene (grooming, bathing, etc.), or will he require assistance?
- Is your parent able to manage her medications (dosages, frequency, refills, changes, injections)? Are you?

Employment Concerns

- Will you be able to maintain your schedule at work and still take care of your parent's physical, emotional, and social needs?
- Does your workplace have a flextime policy?
- Do you consider your work environment to be flexible regarding things such as medical appointments?

Your Health Concerns

- Are you physically healthy and able to provide the necessary care for your parent now and in the future?
- Do you or any of your family members have any special health considerations?

Finances

- Does your parent make sound financial decisions on his own?
- Is she capable of paying her own bills?

Community Resources

- Can you depend on other family members or community services to step in and give you an occasional break from caregiving?

Appendix 3

Tips for Assessing and Addressing Caregiver Burnout

*C*aregiver burnout is defined as a state of "physical, emotional, and mental exhaustion that may be accompanied by a change in attitude—from positive and caring to negative and unconcerned. Burnout can occur when caregivers don't get the help they need, or if they try to do more than they are able—either physically or financially. Caregivers who are 'burned out' may experience fatigue, stress, anxiety, and depression. Many caregivers also feel guilty if they spend time on themselves rather than on their ill or elderly loved ones."[1]

According to the WebMD site, the symptoms of caregiver burnout can include:

- withdrawal from friends, family, and other loved ones
- loss of interest in previously enjoyed activities
- feeling blue, irritable, helpless, and hopeless
- changes in appetite, weight, or both
- changes in sleep patterns
- getting sick more often
- feelings of wanting to hurt yourself or the person for whom you're caring
- emotional and physical exhaustion
- irritability

---

1. *Heart Disease: Recognizing Caregiver Burnout.* WebMD. http://www.webmd.com/heart-disease/guide/heart-disease-recognizing-caregiver-burnout.

Caregivers can take a number of practical steps to address caregiver burnout:

- Join a support group. It's important to meet with others who share your stresses and life issues in a forum where discussion, support, and practical advice are offered.
- Get counseling. Seek help right away if you feel that you're tempted to hurt yourself or your loved one. Check with the National Family Caregiver Support Program for available services, as well as online support groups and programs.
- Find respite through an adult daycare program or through homecare. Check with the Area Agency on Aging to see whether local mileage programs will help cover the costs.
- Schedule time for yourself. Pursue interests, hobbies, go to lunch with friends, indulge yourself with a massage.
- Be sure you have a correct diagnosis and you've learned how to best manage it. Utilize the local library or Internet to keep current.
- Tap into available services in your area. Check with the Area Agency on Aging as your starting point if you haven't already.
- Put together a core team of supportive friends. Utilize the resources of your church, and don't be afraid to ask for help in specific ways (lawn mowing, a few hours of respite, a frozen meal, etc.)
- Protect your own health. Eat healthy foods. Guard your sleep. See your doctor on a regular basis.
- Jealously guard your spiritual priorities. Find a daily time to be in the Word, no matter when you may need to schedule it. Pray throughout the day—before your feet hit the floor, in the shower, in the car, at the sink, and whenever you can schedule quiet times. Be faithful to church and accountability groups.

Tips for Phone Conversations

1. Be attentive to your parent's mental status.
   - Does the conversation flow logically and sequentially?
   - Does your parent seem fixated on particular subjects?
   - Does your parent seem confused or express that he feels confused?
   - Does your parent seem to be overreacting to anything?
   - If so, has this always been the case, or is this something new?
   - Does your parent seem to be under-reacting to something that should be causing a bigger reaction?
   - Does your parent express despair or depression or how difficult life is?

2. Be attentive to the sound of your parent's voice.
   - Is it weak and breathy, or strong and robust?
   - Do you hear tremors?
   - Do you detect differences from the last time you spoke? From six months ago?
   - Do you have to speak more loudly or repeat more frequently than usual?

3. Be attentive to your parent's health concerns.
   - Does your parent explain health concerns in great detail?
   - Is there a new problem every time you speak?

- Does your parent seem to be able to manage her prescription, or are there concerns that dosages are being missed?
- Is your parent falling frequently? Is anyone reporting signs of bruising?
- Does your parent complain about not being able to get out of bed or a chair easily?

4. Be attentive to your parent's eating habits.
    - Can your parent recall what he ate at his last meal?
    - Are you confident that meals are well balanced?
    - Can your parent tell you what's in the refrigerator and pantry? Are the items healthy?
    - Can your parent tell you when the last time food shopping was done and what was bought?

5. Consider establishing a calling circle for accountability.
    - Establish a list of people who live close to your parent who are willing to call your parent on designated days, for instance, Monday mornings or Tuesday afternoons, to check on your parent's status.
    - These people serve as emergency back-up, should your parent not respond to their call. They also provide emotional support with regularly scheduled chats.

A Caregiver's Starter List of Helpful Tasks

Household

- Clean the house or pay someone to do it. Pay special attention to potential grease accumulation in the oven.
- Clean out the refrigerator and freezer.
- Rearrange the pantry and cupboard so items most often used are within easy reach.
- Label cleaning agents in large letters.
- Do the laundry.
- Sort seasonal clothing.
- Clean a closet.
- Make a large-print telephone list.
- Replace low wattage light bulbs with higher wattage if your parent has difficulty seeing.
- Make sure the toilet height is comfortable. Consider buying an extension seat.
- Install handrails near the toilet and in the shower.
- Check the safety of accessibility of the shower and or tub.
- Change the temperature on the hot water heater to 120 degrees to prevent accidental scalding.
- Check that all smoke and carbon monoxide detectors are working and replace batteries.
- Use a marker to highlight the "off" position on stove dials.
- Program the telephone for one-touch dialing, including 911, emergency numbers, and frequently called numbers.
- Install extension phones in all rooms.

- Install deadbolts on outside doors.
- Buy a phone with large numbers and adjustable volume.

Food Preparation

- Fill out a food shopping list and menu plan together.
- Go grocery shopping.
- Prepare meals together and make leftovers for the freezer.
- Purchase favorite foods that might require more involved preparation and have a special meal at home.
- Make a favorite recipe from childhood—yours or your parent's—and share the memories.

Activities

- Wash your mother's hair or take her to a salon.
- Give a manicure or a massage.
- Make calls to friends and relatives.
- Address and mail cards to friends.
- Make out a Christmas gift or card list.
- Make out a calendar of birthdays, anniversaries, or other special events.
- Go clothes shopping or catalog shopping.
- Go through photo albums and label pictures. Consider making your parent responsible for assembling a simple picture album.
- Talk about your parents' family and get help in putting together your family history.
- Ask your parents to talk about their early lives.
- Plant potted flowers or vegetables that require little maintenance or stooping.

Finances

- Review and balance the checkbook.
- Make sure all bills have been paid.

- Review any changes in life insurance policies or medical policies.
- Review financial concerns and budget projections.
- Make a list of all credit cards, their numbers, and their expiration dates.
- Cancel all credit card accounts that are no longer used and cut up the card. Be sure you write to the company and have your parent sign the letter.

Medical

- Make a list of all your parent's medications and when they're to be taken. Post one on her refrigerator and take one with you. Send one to siblings.
- Mark the medicine bottles appropriately or set up a system. Make sure your parent is not getting childproof bottles, which are difficult for elderly people to open.
- Throw away all outdated medications.
- Update contact information and phone numbers for doctors. Sign HIPAA release forms at doctors' offices for release of information.
- Inquire about power-of-attorney documents and desires for both medical and financial decisions.
- Review all medical claims forms and reimbursements.

Ten Tips for Long-Distance Caregiving

AARP.org estimates that more than 5 million Americans are long-distance caregivers. A 2004 study conducted by MetLife in association with the National Alliance for Caregiving found that there is an average of 450 miles between a caregiver and his/her loved one."

1. Communicate as often as you can by phone. Purchase a long-distance plan that allows you to call your loved one as frequently as possible.

2. Use a variety of means to communicate: e-mail, letters, cards, calls, technology.

3. Make the most of your visits. Schedule time with doctors and other professionals. Make sure siblings, friends, and neighbors are aware of your visit so you can talk over your loved one's circumstances with as many people as possible who share your loved one's life.

4. Try to identify your parents' needs and what they may be willing to accept in the way of assistance. Don't make decisions behind their backs.

5. Investigate all resources available for assistance: the Area Agency on Aging, county, city, regional agencies, the library, Yellow Pages, and Internet.

6. Establish a network to help your parents. Identify who both you and they should call in an emergency. Consider engaging the services of a senior companion, people to

help with tasks, people to check on them regularly who can report to you on their progress and condition.

7. Work out an arrangement for sharing tasks with siblings and close relatives.

8. Hire a geriatric care manager or surrogate caregiver, if needed.

9. Consider hiring someone to live-in, being careful to use due diligence in the hiring process.

10. Think about the advantages and disadvantages of moving your parents closer.

Appendix 7

Tips for Improving Communication
with Elderly Loved Ones

1. Adapt your communication style, taking into consideration the effects of life changes, illness, and dementia for your loved one.
    - Speak clearly and distinctly, at eye level.
    - Choose a vocabulary appropriate to your loved one's ability level.
    - Be patient when waiting for responses, and be willing to restate questions and answers.
    - Be sensitive—consider your demeanor, tone, and facial expressions as you communicate.
2. Respect who your loved one is as an image bearer of Jesus Christ. Regard his or her background, values, knowledge, and experience.
3. Create a comfortable and relaxed mood for interaction. Don't place performance expectations on your loved one.
4. For those with memory loss, gently guess and use context clues from circumstances and body language to help interpret intent. It doesn't matter if they communicate precisely or clearly. Gentle, loving acceptance is your greatest gift.
5. As cognitive abilities diminish, place greater emphasis upon providing information for your loved one. Avoid asking questions that require your loved one to provide information for you.
6. Provide links to your loved one's past:
    - Scrapbooks

- Photo albums
- Tapes, CDs

7. As much as possible, encourage your loved one to engage in activities, and participate with him or her:
    - Programs
    - Gardening
    - Reading books and magazines
    - Puzzles and games
    - Walks
    - Manicures
    - Storytelling, singing
    - Scrapbooking

8. Create a visitors' journal, tape, or photo album for your loved one to re-play, re-read, or look through to remind him or her who was there to visit. The journal also provides a wonderful written record for family members who come to visit or to preserve after your loved one's death.

9. Don't be afraid to involve children in visits, but remember that overstimulation can be taxing for older people. Avoid bringing more than one or two children at a time, and keep the visits brief.

10. Physical touch is important. Give hugs, brush hair, hold hands, or offer to give a shoulder rub or a manicure.

11. Ask questions about the stories of your loved one's past, if he or she is able to remember. Be sure to ask your loved one how he or she felt about the memories recalled.

12. Learn to be comfortable with silences.

Suggestions for Creating Shared Stories with Your Loved Ones

*T*he following topics will help you evoke conversations or memories to talk about. Ask open-ended questions about the various subject areas, not just questions with *yes* or *no* answers.

Celebrations: Tell who was there and why the day was special (horrible, embarrassing, heartbreaking, etc.). Have your loved one focus on what aspects of the day made it special for her.

Birthday
Christmas
Your graduation
The graduation of someone special to you
Your wedding
The wedding of someone special to you
Anniversary
Births
Homecoming (someone from war, from a long separation)

Famous Firsts: Tell who was there and the details of the day— what everyone wore, where they went, how they got there, what they may have eaten, what they did after they arrived, how people reacted to these circumstances in those days.

Your first date
Your first job
Your first car/bicycle/motorcycle

Your first kiss
Your first girlfriend/boyfriend
Your first television
Your first telephone
Your first memory of school

Favorites: Tell what about these things are your favorites and why. What made them especially memorable to you? Who would you have shared these memories with at the time?

A favorite place to go on a date when you were young
A favorite family vacation as a child
A favorite vacation you took your own children on
Your favorite aunt, uncle, or special relative
Your favorite memory of a grandmother or grandfather
Your favorite memory of your father or mother
Your favorite teacher
A favorite recipe
A favorite food that your mother or grandmother cooked or baked
A favorite family heirloom
A favorite story about a family member when he or she was young

Life Passages: Tell how these experiences or people changed your life.

War experiences
The accomplishment you feel the most proud of
Your first experience with death
Your wedding day
The person you would most like to see again
Your most significant faith experience
Your most influential mentor

Your greatest regret

Your greatest legacy

Major changes you have seen take place in your life (technologically, politically, culturally)

If you could live your life over, what would you change, and why?

An Average Day: Relate the details of an average day in each of these eras of life.

An average day in elementary school/high school:

What did you wear?

What did you take for lunch?

How did you get to school?

Who did you sit by?

What did you study?

Who was your teacher?

Who was your best friend?

What was recess like?

What did you do after school?

An average day in the military:

When did you get up?

What did you eat?

What were you asked to do?

Where did you serve?

How often did you communicate with family at home?

An average day in 1950:

How did you get to work?

What were you doing for a living?

What was your favorite form of entertainment or recreation?

Who was your favorite politician?

Who was your favorite musician or singer?

What were your favorite television shows (if you had a TV)?

Where did you vacation, and who went with you?

Tips for Communicating with People with Dementias

1. **Be sure you gain the person's attention.** Limit distractions, such as radio and television noise, music, background conversations, or hallway sounds. Identify who you are and your relationship to the person. For instance, "Hello, Phyllis. I'm your daughter, Shelly." Establish and maintain eye contact.

2. **Set a positive tone through your body language and voice.** Use facial expressions and gentle touch to convey positive affirmation.

3. **Communicate simply.** Use simple words and sentences and speak slowly and distinctly in a low pitch. Repeat words and phrases, if necessary, and wait for responses. Rephrase in simple words, and provide information rather than ask questions.

4. **When you ask questions, make them simple, and ask one question at a time.** Ask simple yes or no questions, and provide answer prompts within the question; for instance, "Would you like to watch TV, or go for a walk?"

5. **Provide instructions with only one or two steps at a time, and focus only on the immediate goal.** Provide encouragement and verbal praise.

6. **When your loved one becomes upset, redirect him or her with another activity.** Change the subject or the activity, but first acknowledge his or her frustration.

7. **Be willing to listen and wait.** Silences are all right, and it's acceptable to suggest words. Always listen for the meaning from context clues and body language rather than what is actually being said.

8. **Be generous with reassurance.** People with dementia are lost in a world of confusion. Reality and unreality coexist in their minds. Do not try to convince them that they are wrong, but try to comfort and reassure them. Use verbal praise and touch—holding hands and hugs, stroking an arm or a shoulder.

9. **Don't forget to laugh.** People with dementia love to laugh. Find occasions to laugh with them.

10. **Reminisce.** Remembering the past can be a comfort to those with memory loss. However, when asking questions about the past, ask general questions rather than questions that ask for specific information.

Suggestions for Decision-Making and Compromise

*R*emember that family decision-making will always be a complex process and will seldom, if ever, proceed in a straight line. The following list is a starting point for tailoring to your own needs for your individual circumstances and family culture.

1. Decide on the purpose for the family meeting or the circumstances surrounding the decision that needs to be made.

2. Remember that the more supportive that people who are involved in the ownership of the decision are, the more affirmation is generated for the caregiver and the loved one.

3. Determine the appropriate family members, caretakers, and close friends you may want to involve in the decision-making process. If it's likely that the environment might be tense or you anticipate conflict, consider inviting a pastor or experienced mediator.

4. Whenever health and circumstances make it possible, include your loved one in the decision-making process and respect his or her autonomy.

5. Gather important relevant information beforehand and make sure it's readily available to everyone.

6. Prepare an agenda if a meeting is scheduled. Clearly spell out the purpose for the meeting. It's advised that you not take on too many priorities for one meeting.

7. Be sure you understand the purpose of the meeting (reaching consensus, sharing information, showing support, making a difficult decision) and the roles of those present.
8. Commit to never making important decisions hastily or in anger.
9. When negotiating and considering multiple opinions:
   a. Make lists or charts of pros and cons.
   b. Clearly distinguish between needs (health, safety, etc.) and desires (what I like or prefer) in a situation.
   c. Be creative and brainstorm all possible options and variations of options, working toward the choice that *best* represents a solution for your situation.
   d. Acknowledge that no situation will be perfect. Sometimes close is as good as it gets.
   e. Break the problem into small steps or small parts.
   f. Assign tasks and due dates with a phone call list.
10. Acknowledge where/with whom the final decision-making authority lays.
11. Decide if a follow-up strategy is needed.
12. Be willing to accept incremental change.
13. Be willing to compromise. Yes—you!
14. Be realistic. Don't expect change and compromise to come easily.
15. Bathe all your efforts in prayer.

Vital Information for Caregivers' Ready Reference

Legal name _____

Address _____

_____

All telephone numbers:

    Home _____

    Cell _____

    Other _____

Social Security number _____

Medicare ID number _____

Driver's license number/date of issue/expiration _____

_____

Date of birth _____

Social Security number of spouse _____

Medicare ID number of spouse _____

Date of birth of spouse _____

Location of birth certificate _____

Location of marriage license _____

Location of spouse's death certificate _____

Location of divorce record _____

Location of will _____

Location of checkbook _____

Location of ready cash _____

Location of savings account register _____

Pharmacy name_____

Phone number _____

Address _____

Father's

    Med list (meds, dosages, frequency) _____

    _____

    _____

    Known allergies (drugs and other) _____

    _____

    Medical/surgical history _____

    _____

    _____

Mother's

    Med list (meds, dosages, frequency) _____

    _____

    _____

    Known allergies (drugs and other) _____

    _____

    Medical/surgical history _____

    _____

    _____

Primary care physician's name _____

Phone number_____

Address _____

Dentist's name_____

Phone number_____

Address _____

All specialists' names (podiatrists, cardiologists, etc.)

Name _____

Phone number _____

Address _____

Name _____

Phone number _____

Address _____

Name _____

Phone number _____

Address _____

Employer's name _____

Employer's address _____

Employer's phone_____

Medicare benefits information _____

Medicaid benefits information _____

Pension plan information _____

_____

Primary insurance company name _____

Phone number_____

Policy number _____

Contact person _____

Secondary insurance company name _____

Phone number _____

Policy number _____

Policy type_____

Contact person _____

Long-term insurance company name _____

Phone number _____

Policy number _____

Contact person _____

Life insurance company name _____

Phone number _____

Policy number _____

Contact person _____

Disability insurance company name _____

Phone number _____

Policy number _____

Contact person _____

Veteran's benefits information_____

Phone number _____

Contact person _____

Pastor's name_____

Church _____

Phone number _____

Address _____

Financial advisor _____

Company name_____

Phone number _____

Address _____

401(k)/IRA documents _____

Stockbroker _____

Company name_____

Phone number _____

Address _____

Vital Information for Caregivers' Ready Reference

Primary financial institution _____

Phone number _____

Address _____

Types of accounts _____

Account numbers _____

Secondary financial institution _____

Phone number _____

Address _____

Types of accounts _____

Account numbers _____

Location of safety deposit box _____

Box number _____

Location of key _____

Authorized signatures _____

Name of attorney _____

Name of firm _____

Phone number _____

Location of advanced directive _____

Appointed power of attorney/s _____

Military service record _____

Location of records and honors_____

Location of discharge papers_____

Location of tax returns _____

_____

Location of home deed/mortgage _____

Home equity loan papers_____

Credit card companies
    Card Name _____
    Names of account holders on card _____
    Phone numbers _____

    Card Name _____
    Names of account holders on card _____
    Phone numbers _____

    Card Name _____
    Names of account holders on card _____
    Phone numbers _____

All current service contracts (technology, services, alarms, etc.)

_____

_____

_____

Pre-paid funeral arrangements _____
Location of the plan or contract _____
Name of the provider _____
Phone number _____
Address _____
Location of the burial plots _____

_____

Insurance policies for auto, home, property, and casualty
    Company name _____
    Phone number _____
    Address _____
    Contact person _____

Company name_____

Phone number _____

Address _____

Contact person _____

Company name_____

Phone number _____

Address _____

Contact person _____

Company name_____

Phone number _____

Address _____

Contact person _____

Vehicle titles _____

_____

_____

Vehicle loan/lease papers _____

_____

_____

Appendix 12

Suggestions for Assessing Your
Parent's Driving

One of the most difficult aspects of aging can be the loss of freedom and independence that comes with losing one's driver's license. Consider the following suggestions as you talk through this complex aspect of aging with your loved one.

1. Ride with your parent periodically and informally assess his or her reaction time, level of alertness, interaction to his or her environment, and confidence behind the wheel.

2. Discuss hearing impairment, vision impairment, and other physical limitations with your parent's physician.

3. Resist the urge to be critical, even though you may have concerns about your parent's driving safety. Instead, be proactive and encourage him or her to seek an outside assessment of his or her skill level or a refresher course.

4. Discuss the possibilities of restricting your parent's driving options as his or her mental and physical faculties begin to wane. For instance, you may opt to have him or her fly to long-distance destinations rather than drive. Or you may choose to ask your parent to drive only short distances for shopping or for social activities, encouraging him or her to carpool as often as possible.

5. If you have serious concerns about your parent's safety behind the wheel, ask his or her physician to order an assessment of his or her abilities through the Secretary of State. It's far better to work through the frustrations of a lost license than to grieve the loss of life due to inaction.

AARP Driver Safety Course
$10 for an eight-hour refresher taught over two days
888.AARP-NOW
www.AARP.org/families/driver_safety

Association for Driver Rehabilitation Specialists
800.290.2344
www.driver-ed.org

National Highway Safety Administration
Booklets on assessing diminishing driving abilities
888-DASH-2-DOT
www.nhtsa.dot.gov

Look in the blue pages of the phone directory for your state department of transportation, where assessments for general driving skill, memory, reaction time, and visual acuity may be available upon a doctor's referral.

Suggestions for Overseeing Your Parents' Finances

Start Early

It's never too early to begin financial discussions with your parents. Explain that your desire is to honor their wishes and protect their desires. Be sure to articulate your motives clearly—to know their desires so that you can carry them out as fully as possible.

If you're stumped about how to start a discussion on the topic, the Internet has a variety of scripts to prompt your creativity. Or let your parents know that you've begun your own planning and you wanted to check on *their* desires. If they're reluctant to talk to family members about their affairs, suggest that they talk with a lawyer or financial advisor.

Respect Autonomy

Understand that it's important for your parents to maintain their financial autonomy as long as possible. Taking on responsibility for their financial affairs incrementally makes good sense; for instance, allow them to write out their own checks for as long as possible.

Oversee Budgeting and Housekeeping Transitions

Make sure your parents' budget takes into account their long-term needs in areas like health, assisted living, nursing care, medications, and housekeeping. Consider their physical health and the likelihood of eventual housekeeping assistance, assisted living, and nursing care.

Document and Inventory Paperwork

Be sure that you've carefully inventoried and documented your parents' important paperwork and know where papers are kept. Check appendix 11 for a comprehensive listing.

Encourage your parents to designate eventual recipients for items of special emotional and financial significance to avoid confusion and hard feelings later.

Prepare Legal Documents and Funeral Preparations

No matter how small your parents' estate, be sure they've set up a will or a trust.

Have your parents prepare power of attorney forms, durable power of attorney forms, and advance directives for medical treatment.

Discuss their funeral preferences, as difficult as that might be. Do they prefer to be buried or cremated? If they've moved, do they want their body transported home for burial? Do they own a plot and desire to use it? Do they have specific desires regarding their funeral? Again, remind them that your desire in discussing these issues is to honor their wishes at a meaningful juncture of life when they will not be able to communicate their desires.

Grace and Becoming an Elder

*M*uch has been written about the distinction between becoming an elder and becoming elderly. As you think about the transitions your loved one has made over the decade, it's important to consider the cultural differences that separate the generations and to work toward establishing connection and communication. The following suggestions are points to ponder or to discuss as you consider the desires of your loved one.

1. Respect the richness of a diverse life that has spanned world wars, technological advances, entertainment explosions, and cultural revolutions.
2. Respect the realities of physical bodies that no longer function without pain and inconvenience.
3. Respect the need for autonomy and purpose in life—to know that one is contributing and purposeful.
4. Respect and look for ways to cultivate the gifts, talents, passions, creativity, and interests of elders.
5. Respect elders' desire to remain curious, to pursue learning, to cultivate friends, to maintain connection to a larger group.
6. Respect the fact that elders think differently and share different values and cultures. That fact is not grounds for condescension.
7. Be committed to work toward communication, understanding, and growth among generations.
8. Respect elders' need for honesty and integrity in your dealings.

9. Willingly and graciously receive the gifts that your elders have to bestow upon younger generations.

10. Willingly and graciously make room for elders within your church, your community, and your family as viable and honored members of the body of Christ.